I Was a **BETTER** Mother **BEFORE** I Had **KIDS**

I Was a Better Mother Before I Had Kids

LORI BORGMAN

POCKET BOOKS
New York   London   Toronto   Sydney   Tokyo   Singapore

POCKET BOOKS, a division of Simon & Schuster Inc.
1230 Avenue of the Americas, New York, NY 10020

ISBN: 0-671-02722-0

First Pocket Books hardcover printing April 1999

10 9 8 7 6 5 4 3 2 1

POCKET and colophon are registered trademarks of
Simon & Schuster Inc.

Designed by Laura Lindgren

Printed in the U.S.A.

To Charlie, Jeremy, Abby, and Melissa,
who provide 'round-the-clock fodder
for columns and books,
yet continue to insist that I write fiction.

CONTENTS

CONTENTS

3: Mirror, Mirror, on the Wall, Lie Through Your Teeth • 37

4: I Cook, Therefore I Am • 52

5: Household Hazards • 64

CONTENTS

6: *For Better or for Worse* ◆ 83

7: *The Heart of Things* ◆ 100

CONTENTS

8: Shopping Daze ♦ 117

9: Are We Having Fun Yet? ♦ 132

10: Let's Talk ♦ 144

CONTENTS

11: Holiday Hustle • 162

12: Hang on to Hope • 174

1

Not Even a GIRL SCOUT Would Have Been Prepared for This

Friends and coworkers gave us three baby showers before our first child was born. I had everything imaginable a young wife would need to become a mother: diapers, sleepers, booties, a skid-proof baby bathtub with the *Good Housekeeping* seal of approval, a crib and cradle with pastel printed sheets, a man-in-the-moon night-light, and an entire library of parenting books, including *Potty Training Your Child in Less Than a Day*. I was prepared. Well prepared. I honestly believed that I would go to the hospital, push out a brand-new baby, and instantly become a mother.

Instead, what I got at the hospital was a huge shock. The delivery nurse laid my pink, sweetly scented newborn son on my chest, and said, "Touch him, Lori. Stroke his little back." I—the oh-so-extremely well prepared—froze. I looked at the nurse and said, "You mean pet him? Like a dog?"

In the ensuing months, I learned I was not nearly as prepared for motherhood as I had thought. The truth is, you don't prepare for motherhood the way you cram for a final exam or study for the SAT. Motherhood is a profession that is mastered only through middle-of-the-night feedings, messy diapers, and years of on-the-job training.

I WAS A BETTER MOTHER BEFORE I HAD KIDS

How hard could it be to care for a little baby that has the muscle tone of raw egg whites, doesn't eat real food, and spends most of the time sleeping?

How hard could it be? I soon found out shortly after coming home from the hospital with a seven-pound-seven-ounce baby boy.

Actually, caring for an infant turned out to be remarkably similar to my previous work world of newspaper photography. The baby exploded at unpredictable intervals like Mount St. Helens (the difference being that he erupted at more than one opening). He wailed louder than any police siren I had ever chased and could spray liquids farther than any firefighter hosing down a three-alarm blaze.

I discovered something monumental over the course of the next few years. I discovered a cold, hard truth: I was a better mother before I had kids.

Why not? I had it all B.C. (before children). I had a waistline, pleasant demeanor, the patience of Job, and the wisdom of doctors Spock, Rosemond, and Seuss combined.

True, I didn't have any actual hands-on experience back then. In fact, I'd never once baby-sat a child overnight. I'd never rushed a child with a gushing facial wound to the emergency room and would not have known Bert from Ernie.

Despite my lack of experience, I had a clear vision of what motherhood would be. At the center of the vision was a tidy house with a front porch and a wooden screen door.

The house would maintain a casual, yet orderly, look and continually be full of children. There would be my own children and neighbor kids as well, dashing between projects such as baking cookies, building backyard forts, and studying bugs under magnifying glasses.

In my vision, when my children's energy was spent, they would not whine and thrash about and become quarrelsome little wretches protesting a commonsense nap. No, those were other people's children. Your children. I naively believed that my children would politely request a healthful snack (apple, banana, whole-wheat bread—no artificial preservatives, please) and implore me to read Longfellow while they quietly lay down to recharge their batteries.

And in my vision, if one of my children were—by some fluke—shall we say, disruptive? No problem. Once again, having learned from the mistakes of others, I (the expert without kids) would know what to do. I would calmly and rationally discuss the problem with my child. After all, I would be dealing with a sequential-thinking, logical human, not an Ozark mule. A quiet talk, a hug, and the ugly incident would be neatly disposed of in less than thirty seconds.

I innocently believed that my children would be cheerfully compliant. They would never stand in their high chairs, talk back, whack off three pink peony bushes with pruning shears, or try to sell gravel to the neighbors for fifty cents a stone.

So much for fantasy.

Today, as a woman who actually *has* three children, all of whom shoved peas up their noses, zapped their bathwater with food coloring, and argued that Twinkies were one of the four food groups, I will eagerly yield my role as expert to younger women—women without children, of course. The

3

truth is, this vision thing just hasn't worked out according to the Norman Rockwell scenario. It has definite shades of Stephen King.

Parts of the vision are there. We do live in a house.

But I neglected to project exactly how we would maintain that casual, yet orderly, look. I failed to foresee that I'd be compelled to clutch an extra-large trash bag in one hand and a stopwatch in the other, while barking, "You have ninety seconds to pick up all this junk! Whatever is left goes directly to the mission. GO!"

The porch is there, too. In the summer, two ferns grace the white turned posts, giving it a tranquil appeal. However, the calm is frequently shattered by a crazed woman yelling, "Quit swinging off that porch rail and jumping into the ivy! NOW!"

The wooden screen door is in place as I had imagined, as well. It leads to the garage. (That's it slamming now.) We're on our second one; the frame is splintered, and there's a bulge in the screen.

And true to my dream, there's never been a problem rounding up kids. Day or night, you can wave a box of ordinary, boring saltine crackers out the front door and six kids, three dogs, and one hamster appear on the premises before you can yank the twist tie off the bag. In my view, that many bodies constitutes a small party—or a starter zoo. My children adamantly disagree. They are 100 percent, absolutely, positively, certain there's always room for at least five more. Talk about stubborn.

Actually, it's a great life. It's just not the one I envisioned. It's a wee bit more intense.

Exciting.

Dirtier.

Challenging.

Being a mom is more nerve-racking and more rewarding than I, or any expert, could ever have envisioned.

The bottom line is, I simply forgot to factor in the major difference between romantic visions and reality: Reality comes with audio.

COOL, CALM, AND CRAZY

After having my first baby, I was overwhelmed with a feeling of privilege. I could not believe that on a planet with seven expansive continents, seventeen massive oceans and seas, and more than five billion people, this fragile individual had been entrusted to me.

It was a thrill tainted with a heavy dose of apprehension. After all, here I was in my twenties, young, naive, and totally inexperienced with babies (once I had helped a cousin deliver baby pigs in Homer, Nebraska, but I didn't think that really qualified as a bona fide parenting experience). And then one day, there I was, in complete and total charge of an infant. My lack of experience was compounded by the fact that I was living two thousand miles away from my nearest relative who might actually know a thing or two about caring for a baby.

It is safe to say that, domestically, I was as green as they come. I had yet to discover the power of bleach or fabric softener when doing laundry. I was unable to cook rice without pulverizing it or touch raw chicken with my bare hands without gagging. Yet I'd been entrusted with a baby, a real, live, miniature human being. I wondered if Someone Upstairs had made a mistake.

After all, I was a person with a dark side. I signed insurance policies without reading the fine print. I didn't fix sagging hems with a needle and thread, I stapled them. Or paper-clipped them. Or used masking tape. I parked in metered parking when I ran errands downtown and never bothered to feed the meter. Should someone this reckless really be given the responsibility of caring for a baby?

It had been so easy to become a parent that it was almost scary. There hadn't been any test to pass, no interview, no required reading, certification, or licensing. Yet Life had somehow seen fit to give me—the flake who didn't know the difference between an oral and a rectal thermometer, the gadfly who let out a bloodcurdling scream when the pediatrician explained how a Fleet's enema for infants worked—the privilege of raising a child.

I wondered if someday a matronly social worker with Nazi-like tendencies would show up at the front door, ring the bell, and inform me that a thorough background check had revealed I had deliberately blown off algebra in ninth grade in an effort to become more popular. She would then pronounce that I was academically, culturally, and personally ill-prepared for the business of parenting. "GREENHORN" would be stamped in big, black, block letters across my name on the chart fastened to the old bat's clipboard. She would suggest that, due to the fact that I was in a total fog with regard to my new vocation, I should relinquish the baby immediately.

But nothing like that ever happened. No stranger came. No recall notice was issued, no notification of maternal incompetence. I really and truly had been entrusted with the care and nurture of a child.

You don't take a responsibility like that lightly. It changed my life. I began wearing seat belts. I learned how to cook rice (real rice, not that instant stuff in a box) and make cordon bleu. And while I didn't actually read the fine print on contracts, I worked hard at pretending it was of great interest to me.

The magnitude of the responsibility of parenting was sinking in. I determined to prove myself worthy of such a privilege. I would care for, nurture, and teach this child to the utmost of human ability. There was so much this little fellow needed to learn, and in all probability, I would have to do it in about eighteen years. How could I possibly teach him everything he needed to know in so short a time? Oh, yes, and exactly what was it he needed to know?

Science. Science would be important. Photosynthesis, chlorophyll. He would need to know how to classify animals. Was it kingdom, phylum, order, or was it order, phylum, kingdom? He would need to know some chemistry, math, English, writing skills, literature, and poetry. Good poetry, the kind that rhymes.

WHOA! an internal voice mercifully cried. Yes, of course, I was moving too fast. So I found a spiral notebook and began jotting down notes. Within twenty minutes I'd filled thirty-four pages with a list of 724 essential skills I would need to teach the baby. They ranged from the liberal arts to the domestic arts, including how to rewire a lamp, wash fine delicates by hand, fix the innards of a toilet, and change a flat tire.

Sure, he was only ten months old and occasionally still poked himself in the eye when attempting to get his thumb to his mouth, but it was not too early to start. As soon as he awoke from his nap, we'd start working on his fine motor skills, do some verbal coaching on the long vowel sounds, and work on a few leg lifts to prevent the further accumulation of cellulite in those chubby little thighs.

Exhausted by such extensive planning, I didn't much feel like plunging into the curriculum when he awoke. Instead, I packed him into his stroller and we went for a walk. It would be a short walk, naturally, because the very serious business of teaching awaited us as soon as we returned home.

Out on the front porch he began kicking his fat little legs and waving his pudgy arms at the clapboard on the house. I didn't see anything to get excited about. Then I looked again and saw them, too: Dancing shadows cast by a tall, towering fir tree swaying in the wind. While I was watching the changing pattern of light and dark, he snatched several of the soft fir needles, brushed them across his cheek, and managed to smear some of the sticky sap on his little pink palms.

After bungling our way down the porch steps, we paused again, this time for a closer look at the beautiful blooms on a blue hydrangea. A short while later I guided the stroller back to the sidewalk. His head snapped to the right, and he began pointing and babbling once again. (I made a mental note to focus intensively on his vocabulary; this monosyllable stuff was getting monotonous.) I searched in the direction he was looking and finally caught a flash of brilliant color. It was a magnificent scarlet tanager bouncing from limb to limb high in a maple tree.

Before we reached the neighbor's driveway, we made two additional stops. One was to admire the scalloped leaves of a holly tree with its small, bright red berries, and the other to hear a song performed by Natalie, our neighbor to the south, returning home from second grade. The stop with Natalie took far longer than necessary. She sang. He clapped. She sang again. He clapped again. Sorta. It was one of those overly excited claps where tots miss their hands and end up smacking their shoulders. (Made another mental note to work on his coordination and rhythm.)

By the time we reached the park, the crowd was starting to thin. Still, the baby managed to engage the attention of two overfriendly yellow dogs with large, wet tongues and a crusty old man with a beard and a cane. The old man did a magic trick, pulling a quarter out of the baby's ear. He then proceeded to perform a little finger play and sing-song ditty about "Bumble bee, bumble bee in the barnyard."

We wandered over to the play area and found the sand in the sandbox was still warm from the afternoon sun. We sat and dipped and poured, and dipped and poured, and tunneled with our hands. Nearby, the wading pool barely had an inch of water covering its cracked and pale blue bottom. It was just enough to rinse the sand off our hands, splash around in, and watch a crimson leaf bob up and down on the water, driven by a gentle puff of wind.

Afternoon was quickly fading by the time we reached home. We dallied for a while on the porch, playing peekaboo with the sinking sun from behind the stroller. Finally inside the house, I flicked on a lamp, caught sight of the clock, and saw it was already time to start dinner. Then it would be time to give the baby his bath. Read him a story. Say his prayers. Sing him a song and tuck him into bed.

How quickly the afternoon's teaching time had slipped away. I would try harder to do something productive tomorrow.

WHAT THE EXPERTS NEVER TOLD YOU

I just breezed through another book by an author who claims if you give her a child under the age of two, she will give you back a toddler version of Mother Teresa. Unfortunately, the book was in the parenting section. It really belonged in the humor section.

None of our children was born like a glob of wet clay waiting for us to stamp on a personality. Nor did any of them arrive with a blank tablet patiently waiting for us to write out a detailed script for them to follow. They each arrived with a plan in hand and their brains in gear.

When our first child was born, he immediately grabbed one of the tools on the delivery room tray and removed the wheels from the obstetrician's stool. Our second child was born with her fingernails painted Rosa Rosa Red and demurely asked what time tea would be served. Our third child, when slapped on the fanny by the doctor, smacked him back. Hard.

Life would be much easier if parenting were one-size-fits-all. We cling to the hope that there might be one easy-to-learn parenting technique that fits all children, yet we laugh ourselves silly at one-size-fits-all lingerie. Quite obviously, like children, some of us need more control and support, while others are in dire need of a little lift and some cushioned padding. So why are we gullible enough to think there is one generic formula that will neatly fit all children?

It is rare that a parent can use the same blueprint for two children in the same family. What parent hasn't decoded the temperament of one child, sat smugly savoring the taste of success, only to realize the second child is a totally different make and model? Some kids need a tight rein, and others need some slack.

There are kids you can reduce to tears by looking at them cross-eyed, while others require three swats on the backside just to get their attention. Some kids draw a line in the carpet at least fifteen times a day, perch a Lego on their shoulder, and shoot Clint Eastwood sneers that say, "Make my day."

Other kids ask permission to flush the toilet, never take a cookie without asking and faithfully replace the cap on the milk jug. For the record, I've not personally known any children like that, but I've heard they exist.

We have one child who, for several years, was abnormally cheerful, compliant, and easygoing. If that had been our only child, and our parenting experience had been limited to an eighteen-month window, I'm sure my husband and I would have written a book on how to raise perfect kids and be shouting advice to misfits in a Jerry Springer audience by now.

The fact is, I don't get too excited about books like *Envy Me, My Kids Are Perfect*. I would much rather read books like *I Raised Four Boys and Lived to Tell About It*, or *Down, But Not Out: Survival Strategies for Parents of the Strong-Willed*.

My husband and I have been in the parenting business long enough to know one fundamental truth about raising children: Never be so haughty as to believe your little angel doesn't possess a touch of the devil.

GRUNT ONCE FOR YES

A recent unscientific survey, conducted among women gyrating to set a single grocery cart free from massive rows of twisted chrome and steel, found the emotion most often associated with parenting was not love, joy, or contentment—but chronic fatigue.

Naturally you are wondering, if fatigue is such a large element of parenting, why didn't the experts write chapter after chapter on this all-important subject rather than devoting precious pages to topics like "Herbal Cures for Drooling"?

This is unfortunate, because one of the most delicate skills a devoted parent can acquire is knowing when it *is* justifiable to tune out. That's right, we're talking about giving kids the cold shoulder, the big freeze, the I-really-ought-to-send-for-a-Miracle-Ear-soon treatment. Chalk it up to severe sleep deprivation, an iron count in the negative triple digits, or the plain fact that they have me outnumbered—but there are times when answering one more question could mean the difference between celebrating my next birthday in the free world or in the confines of a quiet little sanitarium in the country.

Plead for a moment's rest, get on all fours, and beg for five minutes of solitude, but as long as your body is still warm, you are fair game. To the child, heart palpitations, body shakes, and the inability to utter multiple-syllable words are merely signs that you are still competing in the marathon called life and thereby qualify for verbal bombardment.

Which brings us to another unfortunate fact. People do judge you by the words you use. The average adult has a vocabulary of three hundred and fifty thousand words and uses about half of those words in everyday conversation. Upon becoming a parent however, that figure abruptly plunges—proving a direct correlation between vocabulary and energy level.

Red-eyed parents of a newborn with colic hit bottom, relying on a primitive lexicon consisting of "Ugh," "oh no," "oh man," "there there," and "hush." Jane Goodall's chimps could form better complete sentences.

Once children are old enough to sleep through the night, the parents' vocabulary rebounds rapidly. Soon their repertoire includes difficult to diagram phrases like, "do it now," "over my dead body," "not in the house," and "did you use soap?"

Once the child is old enough to secure a driver's license, though, the psychologically stressed parents' vocabulary quickly reverts to a central core of "Ugh," "oh no," and "oh man."

Occasionally, an exhausted parent in the grips of fatigue can fake conversation with the child by grunting. A relentless child insists on debating whether the correct name for those disgusting brown bugs under rocks is roly-poly bugs, water bugs, or potato bugs. Forcing out a sporadic "Ah, hu, humm, ooooooooh," at strategic intervals requires minimum lung expansion and may even give the child the impression you are sharing precious quality time.

Wasted parents must also consider whether they can live with the long-term consequences of limited verbal communication. For example, when a child who possesses underwear with the days of the week printed on them asks, "Wouldn't it be easier if they just made January, February, and March underwear?" a grunt is probably sufficient.

On the other hand, "Do we only go potty in paper cups at the doctor's office?" can have tremendous long-term ramifications. It demands vocabulary incorporating complete sentences as well as the phone number for the nearest carpet cleaner—especially when the child has just spent the last fifteen minutes in Grandma's bathroom.

I certainly am not suggesting grunting is an appropriate response to every child's question. For example, when a drained and debilitated parent hears a child yell from a closet, "How long before a dead bird starts to smell?" it would be dangerous for the parent to respond at all while in a fractured mental state. The most appropriate response would be to locate the nearest grocery cart, crawl in, and take a nap. You're going to need your strength.

A TOUCH OFF-CENTER

Something happens to a woman's brain when she becomes a mother. Maybe a little red wire crosses with a little blue wire where it isn't supposed to. Maybe an entire colony of brain cells simply packs up, rents a U-Haul, and leaves the left hemisphere in search of firmer ground. I don't know the particulars, but I do know that a significant brain change does occur.

How else do you explain the behavior of a woman who endures two days of back labor that feels like a semitrailer carrying sixty-four tons of cattle is parked on her lower spine? She is too exhausted to grunt, too dehydrated to pant, and too fatigued to cry uncle. Yet the instant this woman gives birth, she is exhilarated, bubbling with joy, smiling from ear to ear, and beaming like a coastal lighthouse.

There has to be a crossed wire somewhere.

How else do you explain the change in those prissy young things who used to faint at the hint of body odor and squeal at dirt under their fingernails? They have a baby and the next thing you know they're slinging dirty diapers like Nolan Ryan pitching fastballs.

Motherhood does more than stretch a woman's stomach muscles down to her knees. It changes the way she thinks and feels. A mother feels cold, she puts a sweater on her kid. A mother feels tired, she makes her kid take a nap.

13

Motherhood does more than put bags under a woman's eyes. It changes her vision. Others see a gangly kid with crooked teeth, bad skin, and zero self-confidence. A mother sees the attractive, strong, and poised young adult that the child is becoming.

There are other changes that happen as well. A mother's brain mysteriously sprouts a filter that strains out the sass and back talk, but retains the giggles and the laughter. Her clean hands instinctively reach for chubby cheeks smeared with drool and faces streaked with sweat and dirt. Her nose manages to tolerate tuna sandwiches left in lunch boxes overnight and sweaty gym shoes producing toxic fumes. Her body is constantly at war with her mind, which continually tells her she's exhausted. Refusing to listen, she tends to a child with the stomach flu from 1 until 4 A.M., then somehow pries open her eyes and staggers out of bed when the alarm goes off at 6.

Without being wrapped a little loose upstairs, no woman would keep slinging the hash, doing the laundry, running the errands, and doing a million other menial chores that are taken for granted. A woman playing with a full deck would send her family a weekly itemized bill or demand a percentage of her children's future earnings.

Who can explain the irrational things that mothers do for their children? A mother has just that touch of insanity that believes that a child can when a teacher says that a child cannot. A mother has that stubborn streak that runs counter to reason as she believes a child will when a doctor says that a child will not. She is the odd duck who clings to hope when those about her insist hope is gone.

Mothers are an eclectic group of women who have lost a little bit of their minds in answering the call of motherhood. They're women nutty enough to believe kids have potential and crazy enough to love them like mad.

2

The HOURS Are Bad, But the Perks Are GOOD

There's a reason you won't see the job of motherhood advertised in the classifieds. Namely, because it would have to read something like this:

> **WANTED:** Woman with the stamina of a triathlete able to work twenty-four-hour shifts, fifty-two weeks a year, with no sick days, paid vacation, or personal leave time. Candidate must be adept at multi-tasking in the midst of chaos, confusion, clutter, and frequent emergencies. Interpretation skills required during the toddler and teen years. Will not consider women with weak hearts, nervous conditions, or aversions to dirt, pungent odors, and small animals.

That's not a job description exactly overflowing with alluring benefits. It is difficult to describe the perks that accompany the demands of motherhood. For some women, the best reward is a homemade valentine, a dandelion bouquet, or the fact that a teenager is willing to be seen with

15

them at the mall. For me, the greatest benefit of motherhood is often intangible. Some days it's the satisfaction of simply knowing that I was up to the challenge.

UNSOLVED MYSTERIES

Rocking back and forth in a semicatatonic state, I sit here clutching a few precious belongings to my heart: a quilt my mother made, a box of Betty Crocker brownie mix, and a new hairbrush I recently purchased—knowing that in an instant, one, or even all of these things, could mysteriously disappear, never to be seen again. Nothing is safe anymore. Nothing.

Unsolved mysteries, that's what they are. We've lost things before: the remote control, the lid to the Tommy Tippee cup, and the snub-nosed pliers, but this is different. How could we lose a brand-new pair of boys jean shorts and T-shirt?

We've conducted three exasperating room-by-room searches, activated the Neighborhood Watch system, and donned rubber gloves to poke through greasy chicken bones and cantaloupe rinds in the trash. They've vanished into an unknown dimension.

There's nothing left to do but play "Get Inside Their Heads." This is a treacherous game (no prizes) usually attempted only by highly accessorized "live psychics" at 900 numbers. While I'm not a highly accessorized individual, having three children who lose a lot of stuff has given me moderate success in this dangerous field of parapsychology.

In the toddler period, childrens' brain waves frequently operate in the *Squirrel Mode*. Unprovoked chubbos in Disney diapers will suddenly display rodent-like behavior. They seize small shiny objects with lightning speed and swiftly bury them for the winter. They silently amass giant mounds of car keys, earrings, and credit cards, storing them in trash cans lined with shredded paper, dark crevices between sofa cushions, and the toes of snow boots. Other popular nesting sites include drawers or containers that must be pulled open and shoved shut and are no more than eighteen inches above floor level.

Tracking a child in the *Squirrel Mode* who has lost things is not difficult. To find the missing treasure, slither through the house on your belly keeping your chin six inches above the floor while asking yourself, "Where would Mickey hide a present for Minnie?"

Of course, not every missing item will be recovered. I'm personally weighing a popular conspiracy theory. It speculates that when mothers lie down to rest after putting their children down for naps, toddlers everywhere quietly roll out of bed and pad down to the thoroughfare behind the local strip mall and host huge flea markets. If we caught them in the act, we'd find kiosks loaded with gnawed-on pacifiers and missing caps to dried-out felt-tip markers. There'd be pegboards laden with spare keys, half-used Chap Sticks, and hair barrettes without mates. Kids would shriek and scream as they barter stray socks in exchange for lids to Rubbermaid bowls. I'm not saying I buy it completely, but it would explain a great many unsolved mysteries.

Around age six, kids' brains develop an additional wavelength enabling them to lose bigger and more expensive things by entering the *Nature Mode*. Losing silverware and small tools while grubbing in the dirt is blindly justified by a powerful intrinsic drive to commune with nature. Smuggling scissors outside to excavate wasps nests and absconding with camel-hair brushes essential for painting locust shells becomes their sole reason for living.

Naturally, the greater the replacement cost of the implement, the greater the chance they forgot where they left it. Lecture all you want on why pinking shears should never be used to cut old linoleum tiles to line a dirt hole, but kids will only drop their jaw slightly and cock their head sideways like you are speaking in Swahili. Their brains can grasp neither your passion for small tools, nor why your face is turning blue.

The shorts and T-shirt? It took a week, but they were found.

The occupant of the clothes, suddenly obsessed by the need to explore the properties of water, had hastily changed into a swimsuit and stuffed the shorts and T-shirt

... in a dark enclosure
... shoved up against the wall
... at ground level
—the dollhouse.

The scary part is, it all makes perfect sense.

INTERROGATION 101

Show me college coeds enrolled in criminal justice classes and I'll show you young ladies preparing for motherhood.

Not that German Existential Philosophy (also known as Esoteric Thoughts by Clinically Depressed Men with Long Beards) isn't a valuable college course. But rarely, when trying to determine which of my children sawed the handles off the brooms, do I ask myself "What would Søren Kierkegaard do in this situation?"

More appropriately one would ask, "How would J. Edgar Hoover handle these pups?"

For example, a parent hears what sounds like water running from an outside faucet and the following ineffective interrogation follows:

Parent through open window: "Is the water running?"
Child running water: "Yeah."

Parent: "What for?"
Child running water: "I dunno."
Parent: "Are you standing by the running water?"
Child standing by running water: "Yeah."
Parent: "Is the water getting deep?"
Child in ankle-deep water: "Sorta."
Parent: "Well, WHAT'S going on?"
Child: "I forget."

It is at this juncture that mothers with class credits in psychology, parapsychology, or animal psychology would do well to chuck all that and pursue an intensive study of the interrogation styles of our professional men and women in blue and their legendary mentor—*Dragnet* star, Sgt. Joe Friday.

The first interrogation pointer we can glean from Sgt. Friday is to stand up. Sgt. Friday never investigated a crime by yelling questions up a flight of stairs, hollering around corners, or screaming through walls while thumbing through *Good Housekeeping* seated on a sofa in the family room.

Second pointer: Hang up the phone. In reviewing hours of *Dragnet* reruns, not once do we find Sgt. Friday with a telephone receiver glued to his ear, listening to the details of someone's labor and delivery while trying to apprehend a felon by cupping one hand over the phone and shouting, "Stop that! Stop that right now or you're really gonna get it! Do you hear me?"

Sgt. Friday would hang up the phone and ask a general nonthreatening question in a calm manner. "So what can you tell me about the water gushing from the crawl space, son?"

Often, after a story has been repeated several times to a professional detective, or Congressional subcommittee, even your most sophisticated criminal trips up on some detail or chronology of events.

And the same holds true in domestic backyard investigations—major inconsistencies in testimony rarely, if ever,

19

inhibit the subject. Usually by the second time through the story, the subject is (a) starting to believe the lies himself or, (b) weaving such a good whopper that you now believe it.

At this point, if the child has been caught red-handed with ample incriminating evidence, forego the questioning. Refuse to negotiate a plea bargain and do not extend the privilege of making one phone call. Make it clear the ACLU limits its clientele to pornographers and highly sensitive individuals offended by raucous strains of *Silent Night*. Now level the charges.

Make direct eye contact with the child and read the mother's version of the Miranda warning: "You have the right to spill your guts. You have the right to send your friends home so we can converse in private. Anything you say can and will be held against you. But tell it straight the first time and the sentence won't be as stiff as if you try to squirm your way out and pull a fast one. Now start talking. And just the facts."

ACCIDENTS CAN BE PREVENTED

It's the little touches that make a house a home—like the orange cones and flares in the front yard. They're a courtesy gesture warning passersby they're approaching a danger zone. Hardly a day goes by without personal injury or property destruction attributed to mysterious accidents.

Take the dirty handprint above the door frame. It has the distinct marks of our son.

"How did that get up there?" I asked.

"It was an accident."

Hard to imagine how a boy, short for his age, could accidentally leave a handprint eight feet above the floor.

Since the details are slow forthcoming, I'm forced to reconstruct the scenario on my own. My guess is that he tripped over the throw rug, rolled to his feet, only to discover he now possessed the thighs of Spiderman, which—totally and completely against his will—propelled him skyward. Hence, to prevent hitting his head on the ceiling, he smacked the wall with a filthy hand.

But that doesn't explain the "accident" that left a grass stain at shoulder height on the stairway wall, or the tire mark running up the garage door.

Yesterday's Accident of the Hour was when Kool-Aid came within a millimeter of splashing onto slides my husband was preparing for a presentation.

"Why do you think this almost happened?" I asked the child in question.

"Accident, I guess."

"Accident? I thought it looked quite deliberate when you threaded three straws together and began slurping with the suction of an industrial vacuum cleaner."

"Well, it was an accident that the straws didn't hold together too well."

"Repeat after me, Accidents can be prevented. Accidents can be prevented."

Slipping in the tub is an accident. Tripping on the stairs is an accident. Shredding massive quantities of Whitewater documents is an accide . . . hey, wait, that wasn't an accident either. Likewise, running into each other's extended hands, pinching fingers, and pummeling one another with water balloons from upstairs windows are not accidents. They expect me to believe the Bermuda Triangle has relocated to Central Indiana and we are now prey to accidents beyond human control.

I didn't buy the accident line then and I don't buy it now. That's why I want these kids to learn that most "accidents can be prevented." It's become a regular family mantra. It's probably the only thing they will ever remember me saying.

As a matter of fact, I may even suggest they memorialize it on my tombstone:

Here lies our dear mother quite dead,
In our hearts we have lamented,
She didn't give us a dime each time she said,
Most accidents can be prevented.

88 KEYS TO PARENTING

You see them in the malls, the grocery store checkout lanes, and pizza joints. They're the frustrated parents getting tough with out-of-control kids. We've all witnessed the spectacle at one time or another.

It's not pretty watching a grown adult sink to bribing and bargaining with tiny tyrants.

Frankly, I prefer something with a little more sting. Which leads us to the single greatest challenge facing all parents: how to continually innovate fresh and creative ways to bring our own tyrants into line. The number one most effective punishment you can inflict on children is not a scolding, lima beans, or ten minutes in the time-out chair. It's two words: Music Lessons. Isn't it time we admit it?

The sole reason parents shell out hundreds of dollars a year on music lessons is because they love to see their children squirm. Parents relish watching children slouch at the piano bench and whimper, "Why are you making me do this? Why do I hafta practice? Why can't I quit?"

A recent poll of piano students found that 86 percent "strongly agreed" piano lessons are a thinly disguised form of parental revenge. The remaining 14 percent were unable to come to the phone, as their half hour of torture was not yet finished for the day.

Finally, a generation of savvy children now see music lessons for what they really are—parental spite. They even write letters about it to advice columnists.

DEAR GABBY,
I used to be a couch potato who watched a lot of television, read *Babysitter Club* books, and ate tons of junk food. Then my parents made me begin piano lessons. Now I am a bench potato who can sight-read music, play all the major and minor chords, and reach a full octave. Why are my parents so cruel?

Signed, HATES ALL 88 KEYS.

DEAR HATES 88,
Your parents provide a musical education because it gives them a sense of security knowing there is always someone close by who can play "Heart and Soul." Just kidding. You are right, they do it for the joy of being mean. How do you think Chopin, Beethoven, and Mozart became classical pianists? They had vindictive mothers who released their aggression by taking in laundry and cleaning other people's chamber pots in order to purchase pianos, before which they could park their sons and watch them wail. Their diabolical plans backfired, however, when the boys actually took a liking to the keyboard and even turned a few bucks.

If kids want to think tickling the ivories fifteen to thirty minutes a day is punishment, let them. You get a short breather and the budding pianist can't help but learn a thing or two about music at the same time. It's a slick system.

Correction. I should say, was a slick system. One of the finalists in a recent Miss America pageant was asked who had been most influential in her success. She said it was her mother, who made her practice the piano, even when she didn't want to. She smiled big and thanked her over and over. Yes, that's right, on national television she blabbed the great secret that piano lessons are not punishment, but a source of personal enjoyment and an educational opportunity children may one day deeply appreciate—not to mention possibly parlay into a glittering tiara, college scholarship, and cool red convertible.

PRICELESS JUNK

My problem is, I don't know a good thing when I see it. Just yesterday I had a worthless twenty-five-foot coiled phone cord in my hand and was headed toward the garbage when I was intercepted.

"Hey, where are you going with that?" asked one of the kids.

"To the trash."

"Why?"

"Because it's useless," I said.

"Are you nuts?"

Apparently so. I didn't realize the cord could be used like a lasso and looped around the feet of moving siblings. I hadn't considered that someone could use the cord to pretend they were pulling and pulling and pulling a never-ending giant parasite from their nose, mouth, or ears.

It's no surprise I couldn't see the phone cord for the cool, entertaining toy it really was. I had the same short-sighted reaction to the musty rack of deer antlers in an antique shop.

"Why would you want something like that?" I asked a drooling kid with big eyes.

"Oh man, how can you even ask a question like that?"

Just dense, I guess. So dense that I also can't understand keeping a coffee can full of cicada shells, Barbies whose heads are detached from their bodies, or empty Wheaties boxes just because they have Michael Jordan's picture on them.

This morning one of the kids asked where a pair of navy blue tennis shoes were. To call them shoes was a gross overstatement. They consisted of some threadbare fabric peeled back from the ragged form that was attached to worn soles by six spindly threads. These shoes were so bad that George Washington's frostbitten troops wouldn't have wanted them at Valley Forge. I'd sent them to that great retread center in the sky.

"You threw them away? I can't believe you threw them away. I loved those shoes. They were the most fun shoes I ever had."

Great. Those shoes gave her feet the best times of their lives and I threw them in the trash. Figures. I am continually doing crazy things, things that will probably get me locked up one day.

I throw out a large piece of cardboard and they act like I've lost my mind. Didn't I see that slab of cardboard was a fort, a puppet stage, or a sled? The kids look at me like I'm some sicko who would drown stray kittens in the toilet. I would never, ever do that. I gave them to one of my husband's co-workers when the kids were away at school.

I admit it. I pitch leftover Halloween candy in mid-November, remove live bait from the fridge after two days (I'm a patient woman), and stuff dingy, old white T-shirts that have turned an ugly gray into the rag bag.

The way I see it, I'm just doing my part to recycle and keep the flow of stuff moving at a steady pace. The major drawback is this: Whenever the least little thing is temporarily misplaced (a book bag, hairbrush, lizard, car keys, car), I'm the one they look to with an accusing, suspicious eye.

"Sheeeee (sneer when you say that pronoun) probably threw it away. Sheeeee probably pitched it. Sheeeee probably bundled it and set it by the curb a month ago."

Well maybe sheeeee did and maybe sheeeeee didn't.

WHOLE LOT O' NUTTIN GOIN' ON

Feet are pounding violently against the floor of an upstairs bedroom. The downstairs walls are trembling like gelatin cubes, and the window panes are jumping like bacon in a hot iron skillet. My three guesses are hackeysack, basketball with an empty laundry basket, or sumo wrestling.

Imagine my shock when I holler up the stairs, "What's all the racket?"

The answer? "Nuttin."

A whole lot of Nuttin has been going on here lately. I've yet to see the printed instructions, but apparently Nuttin is a physical contact game that is loud, rambunctious, and bundles of fun, judging from the laughter echoing through the house.

Water has been running intermittently in the bathroom sink for twenty minutes. The sound of the faucet at full blast is followed by a soft thud, a splashing noise, and then, wild hysteria, whereupon the process begins again. I rap on the door and ask, "What's going on?"

"Nuttin."

I should have seen that one coming. Nuttin has been all the rage around here since school let out. That's probably because you can play it in active or passive mode, anywhere, anytime, in a group or by yourself.

For example, I walk into a room and observe a pair of eyes riveted to an outdoor magazine with a cover photo of a majestic twenty-two-point blacktail buck overlooking a three-hundred-foot precipice.

"Whatcha reading?"

"Nuttin."

I'm not sure what the vocabulary level required for Nuttin is, but it appears to be a pastime that is accessible to children of all ages and interests.

I pass through the living room and notice a child glued to the television. The viewer is in slouch position with a slack jaw and death grip on the remote. "What are you watching?"

"Nuttin."

Hey, it's not like I was born yesterday. It makes perfect sense to me that some network guru would pick up on a phenomenon like Nuttin, turn it into a television series, and broadcast it at 120 decibels to accent the special effects.

Nuttin is also a popular game for breaking up the monotony of automobile travel. For example, you can be barreling down the road at 65 mph with three kids, see a tangle of arms and legs flying like crazy in the rearview mirror, and know that it's just a harmless, fun little round of Nuttin. Another marvelous thing about Nuttin is that kids are even able to play it in the near dark.

The light from inside the fridge has been glowing fainter and fainter over the past half hour in our darkened kitchen. A low-floating cloud has materialized as the refrigerated air mixes with the heat of the kitchen.

I holler out to the bare feet protruding beneath the fog, "What are you looking for?"

"Nuttin."

At the rate these kids have been hunting down and consuming Nuttin, I sure hope it's loaded with vitamins and minerals.

In some ways, Nuttin is turning out to be a rather expensive diversion. So far it has cost us heel marks on the walls, water spots on the bathroom wallpaper, the rapid disappearance of leftovers, and a few bruised ribs.

I can't remember for sure when the game of Nuttin first became so popular. But thinking back, it may have been shortly after they wore out their other old standbys—Haven't a Clue, Fergot, and Dunno.

BLUE WITH THE FLU

This season's flu is vile. The fever. The chills. The aches. The cramps. The nausea. The bathroom. You know exactly what I mean. Like me, you probably have been tossing and turning in bed at night asking yourself, Why? Why me? Why now?

Why?

Why?

Why?

Did I mention that I personally have not had the flu? I'm telling you now, there's more than one way to suffer. I have been taking care of not one, not two, but three people stricken by the flu.

Sure, the flu's bad, but walk a mile in my plastic gloves and breathe this spray disinfectant before you judge me as lacking sympathy. Laundering sheets day and night and fighting the child-proof cap on bottles of Tylenol has not exactly been a week at Club Med.

There are two nursing dilemmas in particular that I have struggled with over the past ten days: how to determine whether a child is *really* sick, and if so, whether this child is sick enough to see the doctor.

Recently, a child with no fever but a "small headache and scratchy throat" was allowed to stay home from school. By 8:40 A.M. this languishing child beckoned me to her makeshift bed on the sofa. In a barely audible whisper, she asked me to lean close—and affix my signature to two postcards.

They were postcards pulled from a magazine. One signature committed us to purchase porcelain figurine bears that would be conveniently delivered to our home once a month for a payment of only $19.50. The second card was for the "Shirley Temple Collector Music Box 'Heidi,'" a limited-edition treasure, hand-inscribed with your personal serial number (which in this case should be 98.6). We would pay for "Heidi" in two convenient monthly installments of $18.45.

Is this child sick? If she thinks I'm mailing these cards, she is delirious. Is she physically sick? Well, she doesn't look sick and she doesn't act sick. So if I were to take her to school at noon, I would no doubt get a call at one-thirty saying she has vomited and is writhing in pain with a fever of 104 degrees.

There are times when it is easier to nail a fried egg to a tree than to tell if your child is truly sick or merely feeling daytime-TV deprived. The only safe and accurate way to determine if a child is seriously ill is to phone your doctor.

Here are a few indicators to watch for:

- ♦ If the doctor can conveniently arrange to see your ailing offspring before noon, your child will be examined and pronounced the poster child for Vim and Vigor and you will be out a sizable sum for an unnecessary office call.
- ♦ If the doctor cannot see your child until tomorrow afternoon or early next week, your child will be sick. Very sick—with something along the lines of that flesh-eating bacteria.
- ♦ If your child complains of an earache during normal office hours, rest assured it will be nothing serious.
- ♦ If your child complains of an earache late Friday afternoon, minutes after the doctor has switched calls to his answering machine, you should panic. This will be a budding ear infection. By the time the doctor's office reopens Monday morning, it will be accompanied by a strep infection and severely swollen glands, and your HMO will no longer cover your current physician, nor any prescription drug manufactured in the United States.

I think I'm finally getting the hang of this home health-care business, but it's a lot more complicated than it looks. Send 'em to school or keep 'em home? Flat 7UP or bubbling ginger ale? Steam vaporize or cold-air vaporize? Call the doctor or don't call the doctor?

One thing I know for certain: When the school shot is a hard one to call, it is best to err on the side of safety. Children can always make up homework, but they can never take back germs once they've sneezed on the silverware in the cafeteria line.

FUN WITH FERRETS

We are a family who does not currently own any large salivating pets. The thought of a dog is tempting at times. But if I wanted any more responsibility I'd have a fourth child or get a second husband.

Naturally, when my kid asked if she could bring the class ferret home for the weekend, my gut reaction was no. But wishing to be thought of as a warm, fun-loving mom, my mouth said yes.

After all, how hard could this be? The caged animal would be parked in a corner, kick a few wood shavings onto the carpet, nibble on lettuce, and return to school early Monday. I earn the title Very Fun Person and prove to the kids that the Queen of No can occasionally say yes.

The roll-with-the-punches mood first ebbed as we struggled to wedge our guest's cage into the car. This was no hamster or guinea pig who would take up a mere eighteen square inches in the family room. This cage was a suite from the Trump Towers for Rodents. What's more, the occupant was not a round, cuddly puffball, but a short-haired eighteen-inch polecat. It looked and moved like a slinky in extended position. The biggest shock was the ferret's name—Sweet Pea.

They only got it half-right.

The kids claimed everyone gets accustomed to a ferret's odor and proceeded to prove it didn't bother them by hyperventilating, repeatedly sucking in big gulps of air permeated with foul vapors. I sneezed three times, blasted the car's air conditioner on high, rolled down the window, and hung my head out the driver's side like Marmaduke the entire stretch home.

Pretending to be unaffected by the ferret's arched back, sharp teeth, and wily ways, I placidly fielded a barrage of questions.

"Don't you just love her, Mom? Isn't she sooooooo cute?"

I conceded she was "interesting." *Cute* and *love* were out of the question. *Spooky* and *creepy* sprang to my mind, but being a Very Fun Person, I kept them to myself.

"Want to hold her?"

"Pass."

"Ooooooooooh. Are you sure?"

"Very."

Once inside the house, Sweet Pea demonstrated night-time hunting skills by darting under my son's bed. She emerged with a half-empty bag of stale Donut Gems.

"Doesn't this kind of thing bother you?" I asked my son between sneezes.

"Not really. The bag was closed. I don't think the ferret licked them or anything. Why, does it bother you?"

"Of course not," answered the Very Fun Person, opening a new box of tissues.

I made good on my word to be hospitable to the critter, and the ferret was allowed to sleep in its cage (with the door double-bolted) in my daughter's bedroom. I crawled into bed with the "F" volume of the encyclopedia and a third box of tissues for my nonstop runny nose.

Ferrets are known foremost for their ability to hunt rabbits and rats, the encyclopedia told me. And then, a bit of ferret history leapt off the page: Ferrets have been completely exterminated in England. If the British, who tolerate high degrees of disgust in everyday living (i.e., warm beer, kidney pies, and Black Pudding—blood stuffed in casings), couldn't tolerate ferrets, then maybe I didn't have to keep up the pretense of tolerance myself.

At 3 A.M., stumbling to the cabinet for a second dose of antihistamine, I also realized this ferret's coat had the same potency as six long-haired cats. I had a raw nose, scratchy throat, stuffy head, and bleary eyes. I braced for a long, miserable night propped in a near-sitting position in order to remain breathing. Meanwhile, one room away, Sweet Pea was nestled all snug in her bed while visions of rodents danced in her head.

By Monday morning my head was so plugged I had totally lost all sense of smell. That was good. We were able to return Sweet Pea to school with the windows rolled up and the heater on high. That was very good.

All in all, it was not a weekend without scientific merit. We learned a lot about ferrets—their noxious odor-producing abilities in particular. And on a personal note, I learned that proving to your children that you can be a Very Fun Person is a feat that comes with a lot of hidden costs.

CALLING ALL CLOTHES

My best white sweater went to school Thursday. Seventh grade, to be exact.

It took me by surprise when it wandered into the kitchen shortly after 6 A.M., sauntered over to the counter, and put a strawberry Pop-Tart in the toaster. I knew I'd seen that sweater before, but I couldn't quite remember where. Then it hit me: JCPenney, spring catalog, fine-gauge cotton knit; the perfect complement for beige, navy, and black pants.

Yes, I did recognize that sweater! It was *my* sweater, from *my* closet.

It looked especially nice from the back—probably nicer than it looks on me. It was a teeny bit big in the shoulders, but not big enough that I could honestly say it didn't fit. So off it went to school with navy blue pants, a forest green backpack, and a brown-eyed blonde.

It's a peculiar sensation to see your clothes walk out the door on someone else's body.

A younger body.

A smaller body.

A body who, in all likelihood, will never be able to return the favor. Maybe I wouldn't feel so powerless if I had a little leverage in these loans. Say, I could swap my sweater for a pair of her khaki pants. Right.

Like I really want the joy of calling 911 to use the jaws of life to extricate my thigh from the waist of a size 3 pair of pants.

She's got a vest that's pretty nice. But wedging in my upper arms, cutting my circulation off, and having three fingers amputated would hardly be worth the trade.

Up until a year ago, the only thing that anybody around here acknowledged I owned were small appliances and furniture.

It was always "Mom's mixer, Mom's broom, Mom's carpet, Mom's sofa, Mom's dishwasher." Ah yes, the thrill of ownership.

Then, a year ago, my daughters discovered that I had moved beyond small appliances and had been heavily investing in clothing. Naturally, being that it was mine, they helped themselves.

My snow boots lost their tread from all that sledding last December. My gloves and scarf saw more of the great outdoors last winter than in the previous four years combined. My winter clothes were outside twenty times as frequently as my body. They were wet, cold, and frozen stiff. Me? I was post-toasty, sitting inside with a hot cup of tea and the thermostat cranked up to 74.

After outerwear, the girls discovered my turtlenecks. By spring they were hitting my T-shirts. I shopped. I bought. I placed things in my drawer and they disappeared faster than a twin-engine plane over the Bermuda Triangle.

Attempting to get dressed one day, I realized I was down to my bathrobe, a red sequin evening bag, and an old pair of white pants. Not exactly a lot to work with. I put out an all-points bulletin for any kind of top that was navy.

They responded with a pair of tights, a white half-slip I'd forgotten I owned, and a bottle of Mega Magenta nail polish.

I commenced my own search and rescue mission, only to discover that my navy blue T-shirt was out for pizza, my navy blue cardigan was bike riding, and my navy blue turtleneck had been given to charity.

I may be confined to the house in my bathrobe, but at least it's comforting to know that my clothes are having an active social life.

SHAMPOO MADNESS

There's more than one way to tell whether a household has teenagers. The most effective technique is to count the number of shampoo bottles in the shower.

If there is only one bottle of shampoo in the shower, it is a household with children under the age of ten. If the shower is littered with shampoo bottles and smells like a dieter's tropical fruit plate, minus the cottage cheese, it is a household with teenagers.

For many years we managed to eke out a relatively peaceful existence with one lone bottle of shampoo in the shower. It was a plain and simple shampoo—no vitamins, special formulas, celebrity endorsements, or exotic scents. After a good suds and rinse, it would quietly trickle down the drain. The family functioned fine with one shampoo, albeit with unsightly split ends and shameful lackluster sheen.

Today, however, family harmony revolves around our ability to stock and supply dozens upon dozens of scented herbal, fruity, and woodsy shampoos and coordinating creme rinses. Much like designer coffees (Colombian, Bavarian, hazelnut, and cinnamon), shampoo has gone specialty.

I haven't done an official tally, but I am reasonably certain our shower has more shampoos than a porcupine has quills. If it is a fruit commonly used in pies or milkshakes, we have it. If it is a scent found only in South American rain forests or turn-of-the-century Shaker herb gardens, we have it.

Banana Medley shampoo? Got it.

Kiwi and Strawberry Blend? Have one and a spare.

Green Apple shampoo and the companion creme rinse? Couldn't live without them.

I miss the days when one shampoo bottle was sufficient. Not only was there considerably more mobility in the shower, but you could blindly reach for the bottle and know you had the right thing. Today, blindly reaching for a bottle runs the risk of emerging with hair that smells like a freshly baked peach cobbler. The question then becomes, do you comb it (the hair, not the cobbler) or slap on a dollop of vanilla ice cream and eat it?

Heavily perfumed hair does have its upside, however. I am frequently able to have meaningful conversations with the kids without even making eye contact.

"You forgot to take out the trash," I call to the heavily scented steam rolling out from under the bathroom door.

"How did you know it was me in here?" a voice responds.

"Easy," I yell, "the scent of Ponderosa Pine with a hint of wild onions was a dead giveaway."

It is a natural fragrance choice for a teen who is concerned with conservation and the environment, but has no inkling of the energy required to heat a forty-five-gallon water tank when he runs it dry with a twenty-minute shower.

I pass by the phone and immediately detect that someone has been logging time yakking with friends as opposed to doing chores.

"Oh, Miss Tropicana, I thought you were going to be cleaning the garage this morning."

"What makes you think I didn't?" she asks.

"That heavy cloud with the coconut aroma hovering over the phone gave you away."

She's so easy to track it's not funny. Although a reasonably bright child, she is of the variety that takes the "repeat" part of the "shampoo, rinse, and repeat" instructions printed on the bottle a bit too literally, making her an easy find.

The evolution of shampoo has made the job of parenting considerably more pleasant. The fragrances may be overpowering, but it sure beats the days when the only scent they wore was Sweat Au Naturel.

3

Mirror, MIRROR, on the Wall, LIE Through Your Teeth

Mothers impose high expectations on their bodies. We expect that, after stretching major muscle groups seven times beyond their normal range, they will immediately snap back into place. Fat chance. No pun intended.

In reality, those major muscle groups travel half a continent closer to the equator with each pregnancy and have no intention of buying a return ticket. As a result, women become vulnerable—vulnerable to thinking maybe we really can find the perfect swimsuit, vulnerable to thinking maybe that new moisturizer really will erase crow's feet, and vulnerable to every diet, exercise, and health fad that circles around the treadmill.

Oh sure, there are a few women who manage to look great before, during, and after a pregnancy. They live in television land, where fantasies become reality and nine-month pregnancies last all of five weeks.

The best thing I've found to help me cope with this shifting body mass phenomenon is a mirror hanging at the end of the hallway in my mother's house. It has a marvelous distortion that makes me look three inches taller and ten pounds lighter. Mom refuses to sell. But I'm certain that if I hunt long enough and find her the perfect swimsuit and a miracle moisturizer, she'll come to the bargaining table. Every woman has her price.

PREGNANT ON PRIME TIME

There's not a woman alive in possession of stretch marks and used nursing bras who hasn't occasionally felt a wave of envy over the pregnancies and deliveries of women on television.

They're the only pregnant women on the planet who look great in their ninth month wearing aerobics leotards that could be wadded up and stuffed into an empty bottle of prenatal vitamins. (What's not to envy?)

They never get morning sickness, heartburn, or gain seven pounds of water weight from a ham sandwich and bag of chips. Of course, it also helps that your typical television mother-to-be takes only four weeks to carry a baby to term.

There's something else to envy about those women. Not a single one sits around blubbering about how she's so big that she's petrified a painter from Red Man chewing tobacco will stop her on the street and attempt to paint her belly. Why would she? A television mom often doesn't show until twenty minutes before delivery. Even then she carries high and looks like she's harboring nothing more than a small cantaloupe under her shirt.

When something does go awry for a television mom— say, she discovers a dreadful, tiny, spider-shaped varicose vein on top of her right thigh—she is immediately tended to by a tall, dark, and debonair obstetrician resembling George Clooney from *ER*. My obstetricians always looked more like Lawrence Welk. They demanded proof of insurance before handing me a little paper gown. And when I complained of terrible leg cramps they responded, "Wunnerful, wunnerful." A television mom gets immediate and sensitive attention. Her doctor screams code blue and laser zaps that vein into oblivion before the next commercial break.

The most enviable quality of a television mother is found in the dramatic delivery process. I would say "in the delivery room," but most television mothers shun traditional health care facilities. They tend to favor elevators, taxis, offices, and remote mountaintops. Case in point: Dr. Quinn, Medicine Woman, delivered her baby crouched beneath a tree on a hillside while screaming hysterically for the better part of the show, commercials included. Such screaming and carrying on are always remarkable, and I admit that I take a rather perverse pleasure in seeing members of the opposite sex absorb these performances as realistic.

But I'm talking about something far, far more impressive than screaming on cue—makeup. A television mom can be in hard labor for six days and still have perfect eyeliner, mascara without a smudge, and foundation that is flawless. Television moms come out of labor and delivery looking like they just stepped away from a makeover at the Estée Lauder counter. Real moms come out of labor and delivery looking like their hair was caught in a blender and their makeup applied by a paintball gun.

Remarkable as the perfect makeup accomplishment is, a lot of television moms with television infants top even that. Two shows after delivery, the new babies are often nowhere to be seen. Oh, the baby may reappear during the next television season as a toddler, but they have a funny way of disappearing right after birth. I suppose after a fat-free pregnancy, melodramatic delivery, and ninety-second postpartum recovery, a seven-pound bundle of joy is down-right anticlimactic.

BATTLE OF THE BULGE

True, it's not an issue as monolithic as national health care or which Elvis stamp to vote for, but it's an issue every woman who has ever given birth must eventually confront—babies never leave the "equipment" the same way they found it.

It really takes years to assess the bodily damage. In my case, I was either pregnant or nursing for almost the entire duration of the Ronald Reagan dynasty. The eighties were years of chronic fatigue, drowsiness, and forgetfulness. And not just for the president.

I was vaguely aware that sometime between transitional labor with our second child and starting the third child on strained squash, our full-length mirror had developed a distortion similar to those on the carnival midway.

But now my energy is back. I'm no longer surviving on the preschooler's buffet of finger foods, macaroni and cheese, and hot dogs. Instead, I'm masticating real food that occasionally even requires the aid of a serrated knife. I've been at full brain power for several years now and am gently coming to grips with the fact we do not own trick mirrors.

The stark reality is that the effects of bearing children, coupled with a slowing metabolism and the mysterious increased gravitational tug of the planet, has left major parts of my body seventeen latitudinal degrees closer to the equator.

My question is this: How long does a woman keep up the diet, exercise, and personal torture regimen based on the shaky hope that the B.C. (before children) physique is still accessible?

Any day now I expect to see the Richard Simmons *Sweatin' to the Oldies* video run my name in the final credits honoring me for losing 2,355 pounds—the same five pounds 471 times. I'm also considering adopting Renoir's rotund bathers as my new model of health and physical fitness.

A too-thin-for-her-own-good childbirth instructor said women could easily restore postnatal muscle tone by doing isometrics—repetitions of muscular exercises—while stopped at red lights. Yeah, right. Exercising all the muscles that need my attention would mean sitting there long enough to cause gridlock all the way to Pittsburgh.

Just when the choice between thinking thin or visualizing a new fuller silhouette is becoming clear, one of those weight loss success commercials comes on the radio. One man interviews another man about his recent diet.

"So Chuck, how much have you lost now?"

"Well Chip, about thirty-nine pounds."

"And how long has it been, Chuck?"

"Almost twenty-four hours."

Well, excuse me, Chuck, I'm sure it wasn't a piece of cake, but I'm also willing to bet a ThighMaster you've never had to set up a potty training system based on a complex monetary exchange of M&M's, or square off with a jar of super-chunky peanut butter and grape jelly when packing school lunches the night before.

The commercial ends as Chip pats Chuck on the back and compliments him on strutting his stuff in a skimpy Speedo swimsuit.

A former colleague of mine photographed two of the *Sports Illustrated* swimsuit issues. He had the gall to flaunt a huge stack of color prints and pretend the only thing he saw was composition, color, and lighting. I was mesmerized on seeing that there was not one stretch mark in sight and impressed that a woman could run in a thong swimsuit without roaring primal screams.

I'm still on the fence as to how much spandex and self-deprivation are worth fighting the g-forces. But being undecided doesn't mean I'm totally void of convictions. I firmly believe we should have gone with the old Elvis—but not in a Speedo.

YOU CALL THIS A SWIMSUIT?

My swimsuit is a sensible one-piece. It is three years old, has no high-cut legs, plunging anything, or thong design. The only thongs I wear to the pool are hot pink and on my feet.

I wear my swimsuit four, maybe five times a year—underneath a dress-length cover-up. I have two prerequisites for removing the cover-up: either we are swimming more than five hundred miles from home, or I am fortunate enough to find a woman to stand next to who has the same thigh problems that I do.

I'm especially thankful my swimsuit has a lot of wear left in it because fashion designers have some wacky ideas for suits this year. They're still stuck in that Honey-I-Shrunk-the-Cloth motif, where a piece of yard goods the size of a dollar pancake is tossed into a dryer on the Super Scorch setting and left there until it has shriveled to half the diameter of Cindy Crawford's mole.

The skimpy amount of fabric in swimsuits is not new; it's the fabrics themselves that are new—or trendy, playful, and sending a fun message, as they say in the fashion world. No clothing article is ever designed simply to cover your body or protect you from the elements in the world of fashion. Shirts, pants, dresses, and swimsuits are continually sending messages such as "coy, romantic, daring, desperate, or will-wear-anything-for-a-cheap-date."

The message that recent swimsuits send is best described as, "Take a Picture, It'll Last Longer." These trend-setter two-piece swimsuits are made out of vinyl, pajama flannel, quilted nylon, fleece, and black velvet. These are not your typical fabrics known for weathering July, chlorine, and ground-in dirt.

I have a hard enough time peeling my legs from a vinyl car seat when it's a sweltering 95 degrees. It's hard to imagine peeling flesh from a vinyl swimsuit.

One magazine featured a swimsuit that was designed like some placemats we had a few years ago. The swimsuit, like our clear plastic placemats, had been filled with liquid. An abundance of colorful little plastic sea urchins, starfish, and seashells floated freely about in the swimsuit just as they had in our placemats. In a few days, the adhesive seal wore off the placemats, the liquid drained out, and all the little trinkets sank to the bottom one-eighth inch of the placemat. It would be a fashion risk to plan a weekend trip with a swimsuit like that unless you were carrying a spare.

I honestly think these suits are mostly for laughs. Real people who want to shed their cover-up and wear a respectable suit turn to the magazine articles on problem figures. These articles outline body types, their accompanying flaws, and techniques for camouflaging them.

The menu is fairly standard, with skinny, petite, full, plus, and mature figure prototypes. Most people overlap a few categories. Myself, I am short, rapidly maturing, with a few full-figure areas and skinny arms. To adequately address all of my problem spots, I would need a suit with wide straps, a halter neck, a blouson chest piece, a tummy control cummerbund, and a flirty little skirt.

Those extra drapes, folds, and sheaths of fabric would guarantee me a youthful neckline, disguise some sagging parts, dramatically slim my waistline, and take the focus off my legs. Which is all fine and good, with one small exception: With that many yards of fabric in a swimsuit, who could possibly stay afloat?

CRY YOUR WAY TO HEALTH

I find that I cry a lot more easily since becoming a mother (movies, weddings, my son empties the trash without being told). I have always tried to stifle the flow of waterworks whenever possible. Now I read that a psychologist has determined crying is good for your health.

Great. I've been focused on keeping a stiff upper lip when the real key to better health—bawling like a baby—was only a tissue box away.

I have no problem getting with this new program, as my eyes can spring leaks at a moment's notice. But for stoic sorts who may have more difficulty, I would like to offer a few exercises to help get you going.

WARNING: Before beginning this, or any exercise program, consult with your physician first. (Shelling out $65 for five minutes of your doctor's time, filling out scads of paperwork, and trying to get reimbursed from your HMO should be enough to trigger a tear or two as a warm-up exercise.)

Exercise No. 1: After rolling out of bed, stagger to the bathroom and stand directly in front of the mirror. Examine your matted hair, puffy eyelids, and those dark, heavy bags beneath your eyes. Look closely at that wrinkled forehead, those tiny lines etched around your mouth, and that extra fold of skin (affectionately known as a waddle in the turkey kingdom) dangling beneath your chin. Now say out loud, "This is the youngest day of the rest of my life." Repeat six times and have a gentle cry.

There now, don't you feel healthier? Sure you do, which is why you are now ready for:

Exercise No. 2: Stop off at the mall and take five minutes to sit on a bench. See those young fellas with the long, greasy hair, baseball caps so grungy they're slick, and their pants sagging down to their knees? Yes, the ones wearing the three earrings and the Party Naked T-shirts. Now, consider this: One of those young pups may some day want to date your daughter. Don't hold back, let it all out. WAAAAAHHHHHH!

Exercise No. 3: Locate the stub from your most recent paycheck. Subtract the net from gross. Think long and hard about what you could have done with that hefty portion eaten by city, county, state, and federal taxes. Maybe you could have fixed that fender on the car, sent a needy kid to camp, sent your own kid to camp, or started a college fund. Now think about what the government does with your money. Members of Congress, who have given themselves a 72 percent raise over the past decade, receive excellent health insurance for only $78 a month and get free parking at the office and nearby airports. Former representative Dan Rostenkowski, who pleaded guilty to two charges of federal corruption, sat on his duff in prison (sniff, sniff) for several years collecting a $96,497 annual pension made possible by your tax dollars.

Easy, tiger, don't overdo it. They only said crying was healthy. Nothing was mentioned about hyperventilating being beneficial.

If you notice no improvement after trying this program for several weeks, you can always revert to traditional methods of pursuing good health: Monitor your fat, caffeine, and cholesterol intake, eliminate any and all foods that bring you a speck of enjoyment, work out like a dog in some smelly gym three times a week, and always take the stairs instead of the elevator.

A program like that actually has double health benefits. Not only is it mildly effective in getting a body in shape, it's so bleak it will drive you to tears.

ONLY TWO WEEKS TO BEAUTIFUL

What do women want? Women want to float in a cloud of lingering fragrance. Women want smooth, porcelain skin, full lips, and long, thick eyelashes. Above all, women want to cling to large pieces of furniture while wearing tight dresses with deep slits.

At least, that's what all the advertisements would have you believe. Hark, the gilded merchants sing: "Wear the fragrance he'll never forget," "Look prettier overnight," and "Lose twenty pounds by Christmas."

Right. And I also believe that a short, obese guy in a red suit is able to slide down chimneys.

Yet, there's a spark of curiosity that makes me wonder if such miracles might indeed occur. Is it remotely possible for someone who has been accruing frequent rider miles on the Sugar Train Express since Halloween to lose even five pounds by Christmas? In this season of boundless hope, goodwill to all, and free fudge samples, the impossible somehow sounds believable.

These illogical thoughts are cultivated by the same brain patterns that have nurtured the likes of Santa Claus and Jack Frost. It's that same section of the brain that works overtime when I pick up a bottle of makeup, read that "exclusive time-released chronospheres deliver an alpha-hydroxy acid, plus skin nourishers," and embrace it as scientific truth.

Some of this year's cosmetic advances are so high-tech as to verge on frightening. Take this one about a lipstick: "Increases lip moisture 350 percent after just one colorful application." If you applied the lipstick four times in one day, that would increase lip moisture 1,400 percent. What would Pink Poinsettia lips do with all the excess moisture? Spit like a ballplayer? That's hardly a Kodak moment.

I am convinced that even lipstick that makes you drool would be marketable this holiday season as long as it bore a French name. Everything sells better in French: *exfoliance* (abrasive soap that rubs off dead skin cells), *tonique douceur* (liquid that dries up nose grease), or *rouge superbe* (color for cheeks so you don't look anemic).

Never mind that many cosmetic and fragrance labels require a translator. What matters is that we think these products are used in France, where thin women sip mineral water and nibble crusty bread at sidewalk cafés while luring swarms of men with dark eyes, custom-fit sport jackets, and fast cars.

French names are so popular that I'm considering one as part of a personal makeover. "Lori Borgman" sounds like a bowling ball dropping from the grip of a novice. Consider "Yvette duBois." I dare the receptionist to say my husband can't be found when Mademoiselle Yvette is waiting on the line. Even this book would have a certain ambiance if the author were named Yvette. Insights about breakfast cereal and upper arm flab would leap from the page like airy prose too heavenly to be defiled by common white paper.

Of course, women can't be fooled merely by a pretty name. Guarantees and statistics are essential, too. At this moment, as your face is dehydrating, each major cosmetic line offers a moisturizer guaranteed to defy age, reduce wrinkles, and produce smoother skin within fourteen days. Theoretically speaking, if a woman switched to a different moisturizer every two weeks (each one guaranteed to produce visible results within days), she should have skin as smooth as a baby's bottom by New Year's Day. She should also have major credit card debt.

Do women really want to be gifted with the skin tone of a preteen, glossy lips, and doelike eyes? Does Rudolph guide the sleigh? It's good work if you can get it, but it's out of reach for most.

What this woman really wants is assurance that my loved ones will look first to my heart, not my spreading crow's feet and deepening smile lines. I also want a new lipstick with moisturizer, but not one that makes me drool. Yvette has too much class to lick her chin.

DRIVEN TO DIET

Talk about the ultimate diet. Eat everything you want and still lose weight. No deprivation, no exercise, just burn calories through sheer nervous energy. It's called the Teaching Your Teenager to Drive Diet Plan.

The weight loss begins by climbing in the car with your soon-to-be sixteen-year-old child. You take the passenger seat, while the kid you still have to tell three times to shut the refrigerator door slides in behind the steering wheel.

Feel your heart accelerating? It should.

I personally begin my driving workout by reminding my son that driving is an enjoyable experience. "Driving a car is a great way to see the world and it takes you one step further toward independence. There's nothing to be nervous or excited about. Just relax, be confident, and you'll do great. And one more thing—never, never forget for one second that this two-ton hunk of cold metal can kill you in a heartbeat. Ready for our safety check?

"Motor under the hood?"

"Check," he says, rolling his eyes.

"Flares and first aid kit?"

"Check," he says, with a sigh.

"Air bags connected?"

"Mom, is this really necessary?"

"Absolutely. Sun visor that says 'HELP'?"

"Check."

After reading aloud the day's newspaper clippings on auto accidents in a three-state area, I am sweating bullets and have lost one-and-a-half pounds before he even puts the key into the ignition. It would take me at least thirty-five minutes of the Kathie Lee workout video to get the same results.

Once the motor turns over, my heart is beating at a low-impact aerobics level. I clutch the door handle with a white-knuckle grip and begin talking him through: "Foot gently on the accelerator. Depress it easy, easy. Now straighten the wheels. Hands at ten and two. Good. You're doing fine, now ease off the accelerator and tap the brake. Harder. Harder! BRAKE, BRAKE, BRAKE!!!"

Beads of sweat roll down my forehead, my hair is wet, and my back is drenched. The workout is proceeding so well that I sincerely regret not having had that hot fudge sundae the night before. We are now at the end of the driveway.

Once we're out on the street, he hugs the passenger side of the road, coming within millimeters of clipping mailboxes whizzing by my face. My pulse rate climbs to 170. With each approaching mailbox, I thrash against my seat belt and arch my back toward the center of the car. My high school gym teacher used to call this same movement a great waist whittler.

Calories continue to melt away as I tell him to turn on the blinker and the next sound heard is "whomp, whomp, whomp." Windshield wipers are dragging across a dry windshield. I tell him to hit the brake; he accidentally punches the accelerator and meekly says, "Oops. I guess I got them confused." I have now burned off at least 750 calories in stress and have visions of lasagna for dinner followed by strawberry cheesecake.

My son and I have completed our first driving lesson/diet plan in a breezy fifteen minutes. I feel as limp as a wet noodle and am having difficulty speaking when my son says, "Don't take this the wrong way, Mom, but I'd rather have Dad go with me next time."

"Why would I take that the wrong way?" I rasp and use the last ounce of strength I have to give his head a playful tousle. "I was thinking the same thing myself. Your old dad could stand to take off a few pounds, too."

WALKIN' AND GAWKIN'

So here I am at home without a car, when I discover I need a few items from the grocery to put the finishing touches on dinner—meat, vegetables, and a gallon of milk.

I do the only sensible thing and walk to the store. A walk to the store is no big deal, as this is a pleasant neighborhood with sidewalks and tree-lined streets and corner stop signs where one out of four drivers still feels compelled to slow down to 65 mph before barreling through.

The only real peril in walking to the store is where the sidewalk ends. It ends at the curb of a busy four-lane thoroughfare bordered by a fire station, two gas stations, and three strip malls. A street like that attracts a lot of demented drivers with lead feet and blurred vision.

Ready to cross, I scout the traffic flow and changing lights. I nearly make it across one lane when a white sedan peels out in front of me. Reasonable error in judgment for any driver whose eyeballs hang down to his tongue as a result of bass so deafening that it vibrates the hood and trunk of the car.

As the sedan roars away, I again attempt to cross the street. A red pickup truck tears out from a gas station and takes a run at me. I do what every pedestrian in our neighborhood does when being gunned down by a two-ton truck. I make a run for the grassy median strip, which in this playful game of street tag not only divides the four lanes of traffic but is universally recognized as home base. The driver of the pickup truck grins and waves. I smile and shout, "Better luck next time!"

Suddenly, cars swerve and abruptly pull to the side of the road. Motorists turn on their flashers. Something is parting traffic more dramatically than Moses split the Red Sea. Funeral procession? Ambulance? A family of ducks?

No. It is a young lady approximately eighteen years old with very long, wavy, blond hair and even longer legs. She is wearing short shorts, sandals with five-inch heels, and one of those itty bitty shirts that looks like it shrunk in the dryer and should be returned to the point of purchase for a full refund. Motorists are clearing a swath in case the young lady would like to cross all four lanes without tempting fate.

Well, what am I—invisible? Obviously not. Two guys at the car wash are yelling at me to move. Seems I am blocking their view of the chick.

I ask myself, "Is this what America has come to? Beauty before age? Courtesy and respect given to a svelte and lanky tart on stilts over a mother of three in sensible flats?" You better believe it.

Which is why my only hope of getting to the other side of the street is to catch up with the dish and cross in her shadow. She is strolling along at a leisurely pace in slow motion to maximize her bounce quotient. I am sprinting at top speed, feeling acute cramping in my right side. Nonetheless, my low-to-the-ground knees are no match for her leggy gams.

The dish loses me in her dust and safely crosses the street amid a chorus of honking horns and cheering motorists. I am still stranded on the median once again reduced to playing dodge car.

Life in the pedestrian lane isn't bad as long as you are young, good-looking, and mostly naked. But if you're middle-aged, have fallen arches, and wear enough clothing to protect yourself from skin cancer, where the sidewalk ends can be a very dangerous place.

4

I COOK, Therefore I AM

I work at home. My computer is strategically located around the corner from the kitchen, which is to say I am never far from food. Some smart aleck kid recently tacked a sign to the back of my desk chair that says, "If not here, try the refrigerator."

It's true. Food is my life. Food is the most frequently used tool in my maternal bag of tricks.

By stocking a fair amount of foodstuffs and overseeing their preparation and distribution, I am able to lure children from their rooms and my husband from the television with a mere crack of the oven door. By popping open a two-liter and rustling a bag of chips, I am immediately everybody's new best friend. By merely mouthing the word *pizza,* I can command the entire family's full attention.

If you want to talk to a mother about power, talk food.

"WATTSFIRDINNER?"

There are three great questions every human being asks throughout the course of a lifetime: "Where did I come from?" "Why am I here?" and "Wattsfirdinner?"

I never dreamed that answering Question No. 3, "Wattsfirdinner?" would be such an integral part of my life.

Struggling to answer "Wattsfirdinner?" allows women these days to connect to a ritual that dates as far back as the ancient Greeks—hanging in the cupboard between 5:30 and 6 P.M., kicking yourself for not butchering a lamb the night before.

Of course, the major difference between us and the ancient Grecian woman is that when she hung in her primitive cupboard, she faced the grim prospects of making skillet magic with only a few dried figs and grape leaves. She also faced the danger of catching her long skirt on fire while working over an open flame.

Not to mention the stress of small children jumping on the back of her sandals, chanting (to the tune of "La Cucaracha") "We won't eat goat cheese, we won't eat goat cheese! No, no, no, no, no, no, no!"

We've come a long way, baby. Today I swing open my twentieth-century cupboard door and face down one box of strawberry gelatin, two boxes of spiral macaroni and cheese—and three miniature Roman candles, remnants from the Fourth of July. And they called Anne Sullivan a miracle worker.

Personally, I thought there'd be more to family life than dinner. But that's what I get for going to college in the seventies with people like Jeanie and Tom, who moved to the Pacific Northwest with no money or jobs. They announced they wouldn't need food because they planned to "live on love."

People said stupid things like that all the time in the seventies and other people just stood by, munching granola, nodding their heads, and saying, "For sure."

We now know such occurrences were the result of diets including excessive amounts of alfalfa sprouts and tofu. Frankly, my children are not amused when they ask, "Wattsfirdinner?" and I say, "I don't know, why don't we live on love?" They are definitely products of the nineties. For sure.

The truth is, I don't have any good ideas for dinner. I've been stuck in a two-track rut that alternates between ground beef and chicken with your basic potato, rice, or tomato-sauce variations.

It's the dinner doldrums, a debilitating seasonal phenomena that occurs several times a year and leaves me completely uninspired in the kitchen, void of imagination, and bereft of any Betty Crocker brain cells.

It's painful to acknowledge that I am a grown woman with all the modern conveniences, such as chocolate toaster tarts, aerosol cheese, and meat as thin as onion skin (no fat, only ten calories a slice), yet I can't think of what to throw on the table by six. Please, don't suggest cookbooks. They're worthless, too. I always end up in the dessert section.

I did feel a faint spark of culinary creativity return last night. I served the chicken and rice with the miniature Roman candle shooting out the bird's chest cavity. It may not have been up to Martha Stewart's standards, but it's a start.

Which all just goes to prove the greatest universal truth about dinner—the truth that supersedes all principles of nutrition, food presentation, and marinades: It really doesn't matter "Wattsfirdinner?" If you make it, they will come.

FIELD OF GREENS

Four, three, two, one... the chicken chunk spirals into the skillet, bounces high, ricochets off a green pepper wedge, and sails smack into the center of a curled bean sprout. What a shot! Two points for the chef!

Many men are more comfortable tackling a two-legged opponent than a four-course meal. But with a little retraining, the male obsession with free throw percentages and zone defense can be converted into the female's home field advantage.

You will be pleased to learn that test kitchen experiments have found it is indeed possible to teach men to cook by using sports metaphors. They can, with little effort and no padding or protective gear, be routed from a Field of Dreams to a Field of Greens.

By way of example, let's replay our sizzling stir fry. We first announced to our athlete that he had been appointed acting basketball commissioner. His first job was to place six green onions on a cutting board and, using a sharp knife, quickly divide them into twenty-nine NBA teams. Faster than you could scream "Foul!" he repeated the procedure for the celery, zucchini, and chunks of meat.

We join the game already in progress to find our male in the final quarter of the Gillette Skillet Playoffs at Market-Shop Arena. One minute to go, and the players zigzag up and down the Teflon-covered court with lightning speed.

Seconds to go, and the coach has his V-neck apron rolled up around his midriff. Great beads of sweat tumble down his brow as he screams himself hoarse. The vegetables are hot, dripping in a tangy soy sauce furthering that home field advantage. The final buzzer sounds, and voilà! Dinner's ready.

I know, you're thinking, "Time out, time out!" You're asking, "Isn't it dangerous to let a man who thinks the four basic food groups are pregame snacks, halftime snacks, after-game snacks, and tailgate parties, handle food that is not wrapped in cellophane?" You're wondering, isn't it a felony to let a guy who believes the Healthy Heart diet means alternating among pan-fried, deep-fried, and oven-fried, loose in the kitchen? Probably, but show me a sport without risk. Okay, show me one besides golf.

Even complex forms of the culinary arts, such as yeast cinnamon rolls, may be executed successfully by a sports-minded guy. The key players—flour, yeast, water, and salt—are mixed in a bowl where the cook uses his hands to skillfully execute Greco-Roman wrestling moves. Clawing the ingredients, he twists the mix in a half nelson, yanks it into a vice-grip, working his way into a full nelson, before cinching the match by trapping the dough in a headlock.

Our Kitchen League rookie throws a towel over the dough and lets it rest in a warm place while he catches his breath and gulps down Gatorade.

The bell clangs, signaling Round Two. The cook returns in fine form, light on his feet. He now approaches the dough like a prizefighter swinging for the title. He punches hard with a solid left, a quick right, and undercuts with a left. He pummels the opponent for five minutes.

Back to his corner, a light dusting of flour on the hands, a quick spray of Pam on the baking dish, and he's back for more. He leads with a hook, follows with a strong right, over and over and over he pounds the dough. Has he no mercy? Is there no end? Wait! What's this? The dough is down for the count. Eight, nine, ten. We have a champ. Knead we say more?

Our athlete now rolls the dough out into the shape of a football field and prepares the field for play by designating yard line markers with cinnamon, sugar, and butter at appropriate intervals. The ball, or raisin in this case, is placed in play on the opponent's 2-yard line. Slyly tucking the raisin under the dough, the coach rallies the entire offensive line and orders the team to advance the length of the field. There's no defensive lineman too big, no butter chunk too slick to stop them now! They're on the 20-yard line, the 10, 5, AND TOUCHDOWN!

Our cook instinctively pats the length of the dough firmly along the seam line. Finally, he slices the dough the width of concession stand hot dogs, turns on the heat (350 degrees), and lets the clock run out for two quarters.

As the buzzer sounds, hordes of fans appear to sample warm homemade cinnamon rolls and give major-league praise to the proud athlete who so valiantly faced the challenge. Don't applaud. Just do the wave.

JUST GRILL IT

If Martha Stewart were a man, she wouldn't have a television show, a magazine, or a single book. That's because she'd have one short, pat answer to every cooking and entertainment dilemma known to the human race: Grill it.

A few men may enter a marriage with the ability to fry chicken, make Belgian waffles, or whip up an ethnic dish or two, but most men enter a marriage with little more than a used charcoal grill and a blackened flame-retardant mitt.

Personally, I should have been suspicious when my husband-to-be asked if the bridal registry had a section for grill accessories. Eighteen years later we still think differently when it comes to cooking for a crowd. He thinks all get-togethers are best conducted in a cloud of smoke and ball of flames.

"I'm having a baby shower for your sister Saturday. What do you think of this fruit torte?" I say.

"Can you grill it?" he asks.

"Great Aunt Etty's funeral is Tuesday. Since we live close to the funeral home, I thought afterward we'd invite the family..."

"Say no more, I'll get the grill."

The male fixation with barbecuing is most likely one of those primal instinct things. I would ask the men who live nearby for confirmation, but right now three of them are busy barbecuing at their respective backyard grills. At least I think they're barbecuing. It's hard to tell; all I can really see are their legs and feet protruding beneath clouds of thick, swirling smoke.

If pressed against the barbecue fork tines, the majority of these smoke-scented men probably would admit that they think women waste time leafing through cookbooks, planning menus, shopping, and preparing foods the night before when we could simply do it their way—"just throw something on the grill." To the male mind it doesn't matter if you are cooking for a group of five or fifty; when you "just throw something on the grill," the meal is complete. Done deal. Divine fiat. Mission accomplished.

I'm all for throwing something on the grill, but when that slab of meat comes off the grill it does not make a meal by itself. I'd simply like to point out that potato salad, baked beans, and brownies do not spontaneously combust into existence. Plates, glasses, and silverware do not drop out of the sky. Carrots and celery left in a darkened fridge overnight do not miraculously breed attractive relish trays with parsley sprigs.

I'm appreciative of men willing to fire up a grill. I do not overlook the grandeur of the gesture (it would be pretty hard to when flames are shooting eighteen feet into the air). It's not that I get resentful when everyone else is outside gathered around the grill laughing and dodging smoke while I'm racing side dishes, condiments, and napkins from the kitchen to the patio. I'm not even remotely jealous when everyone oohs and aahs over a piece of meat that took a total of three minutes to sear, while my delicately seasoned, tenderly marinated pasta salad is totally snubbed.

The last thing I want to do is turn this into a contest. I merely want acknowledgment that there's more to a cookout than a bag of briquettes and a half gallon of charcoal starter fluid.

But just for the record, I'll put my fruit pizza with the walnut cookie crust up against a charred burger any day of the week.

MISDEMEANOR RECIPES

Don't flag down a squad car, but I think I just committed a crime. Not a big crime, probably a misdemeanor at worst. Maybe there's no law against it at all, but it sure felt illegal.

A friend has asked for my sugar cookie recipe. Right above the part where I wrote: Cream: 1 C. sugar, ½ C. Crisco, and ½ C. butter (not margarine), I felt the need to write a title.

Every recipe needs a title, and it is also nice to know where the recipe came from. My dog-eared recipe card says "Mom's Sugar Cookies," but I can hardly write that since I am not my friend's mom. All of which I tell you to explain how I fell upon this flour-dusted path of ill-repute. In the space for a title I wrote "Lori's Sugar Cookies."

That was a lie. This is not really my recipe; it's not really my mom's recipe either. My mom got it from a friend, who got it from her daughter, who got it from a dietitian who used to work for a state hospital.

Perhaps a more upright and honest cook, as opposed to a petty criminal with a wet dishtowel slung over her arm, would put all that at the top of the recipe card. But I had a difficult enough time squeezing in: Add 1 egg. Next, add 1 tsp. vanilla, ½ tsp. soda, ½ tsp. cream of tartar, and ½ tsp. salt. Add 2 C. flour.

So, whose recipe is this anyway? I'm not sure, but I'd rather answer that question myself than before Judge Judy. As near as I can count, it has passed through at least five different recipe boxes on the way to mine, which I believe makes it, as they say down at the station, "hot."

Which reminds me: Roll dough into balls the size of walnuts, dip into sugar, flatten with fork on cookie sheet, and bake at 350–375 for 8–10 minutes. (Add nuts or coconut if desired.)

Last Christmas I made "Jane Ashcroft's Missouri Candy Canes." Jane happens to be married to John Ashcroft, a senator from Missouri. As I was making the candy canes, which became far more time-consuming than I anticipated, I began to wonder how the busy wife of a senator ever found time to create a cookie that required so much time in the kitchen. Or did she? Was it really Jane's recipe or was it her Grandma Betty Crocker's recipe?

I have a recipe on my windowsill waiting to be filed that says "Macaroni and Cheese—Becky." It's incredibly fattening and kids love it. No offense to my friend Becky, but I seriously doubt she ambled into the kitchen one morning with three small children clinging to her legs and said, "Today, just for kicks, I will create an original macaroni and cheese casserole."

I think Becky, too, may have committed a small crime. Don't get me wrong, I'm not saying what Becky did was any worse than what I did, although her recipe *was* for a main dish and mine *was* only for a cookie and I certainly hope Judge Judy will take that into account.

I am simply wondering how anybody can legitimately lay claim to any recipe. For example, I have a recipe for chili from the Hard Rock Cafe. If I double the amount of chili powder and cut the green peppers, does it then become Lori's Hard Rock Chili?

Maybe it's time all those who swap recipes to admit to being accomplices in the steamy world of insider trading. I don't have time to stew over this anymore right now. I have a bake-off contest form to fill out and get in the mail by midnight. I'll think about all this again later. When I'm locked up in solitary.

BROWNIES SPOKEN HERE

I used to believe that the most important language spoken between a parent and child was the language of love. I now know that I was wrong. Very wrong.

The language of food is what most effectively binds my children's hearts to mine. I know that is true based on the following observations:

- My kids love spending time with me—at the grocery store.
- They're keenly interested in what I'm reading—when it's a cookbook.
- They always ask how my day has gone—and if I made anything good to eat.

Food has definitely become their first language. It is woven into their greetings—"Hi, what's to eat?" It punctuates their goodbyes—"See ya, we're outta chips!"

Food permeates their conversations—"There wasn't any fruit in my lunch today." It's the cornerstone of all urgent declarations—"The peanut butter's gone!"

Our most philosophical discussions usually revolve around food: "There's nothing good to eat," says a torso and pair of legs hanging out of a packed cupboard.

"We have apples, oranges, and whole wheat bread," I respond.

"Yeah, but there's nothing good to eat."

"Define 'good,'" I challenge.

"You know, pizza, crackers, cookies."

"Oh, you mean foods from the chemically processed, high-octane, saturated-fat food group?"

"M-U-T-H-E-R! You know what I mean."

I don't know what they mean. I do know if I want to hold their attention, I'd better be holding a brownie. I do know if I want to lure them to the kitchen, the fastest way is to splash vanilla on a hot stove burner (it smells like cookies baking). I do know the only time I can routinely count on good eye contact and clear articulation from them is when they are giving me their burger and fry orders in the drive-thru line.

Food is the framework through which they see all of life. One of them recently asked if we'd ever thought about an addition to the house—a walk-in pantry so we'd have more room to store cereal in bulk. Food is so central to their existence that one of them actually measures important events in relation to the last time he had homemade waffles. Not surprising. That is the same kid who asks what's for dinner while he's still eating lunch.

Learning that my relationship with my kids is now built upon a cornerstone of nachos, bagels, and soda pop doesn't bother me. What bothers me is realizing how rapidly that cornerstone can be consumed.

When the planets are in alignment and my hormone balance just right, I can whip up a decent dinner and have it on the table in twenty minutes. The kids can eat the meal, clean out the serving bowls, and return their dishes to the sink in the time it takes me to leave the table and walk five steps to the stove for the salt and pepper.

When a meal is devoured that fast, a cook has to ask herself what's the point in taking it out of the pan? We might as well huddle at the stove with knives and forks and eat right out of the skillet.

What further amazes me is how well their eye-hand coordination works when it comes to eating, but how unreliable it is when it comes to simple tasks like picking a wet towel up off the bathroom floor or flipping off a light switch when leaving an empty room.

Ah, the mysteries of adolescence.

5

Household **HAZARDS**

The single most deadly "phrase" for any man or woman struggling to keep a household running efficiently has to be *do-it-yourself.* My husband and I have fallen prey numerous times.

I was duped by the Weekend Garden and Canning Project that was to save me time at the store shopping for fresh vegetables, not to mention a whole wad of cash. The project would have worked great—if I had had seven days to every weekend. My husband was taken in by an illustrated *Handyman's Home Repair* book that guaranteed he could fix a plumbing problem in the upstairs bathroom. The details aren't important (so he insists), but let's just say the do-it-yourself repair job mushroomed into such a large-scale disaster that at one point we considered sticking a sign in the front yard that said "House For Sale, As Is."

I suppose it's a hint you've stretched beyond your do-it-yourself abilities a few too many times when the kids see you pick up the toolbox, drop to their knees, and begin pleading, "Please, please, call a professional!"

THE GREAT APPLIANCE REBELLION

There's nothing like entertaining to bring out the dark side of your kitchen appliances. You can count on the stove, refrigerator, and garbage disposal to hum along smoothly when you're eating on paper plates and just feeding the family. But the minute you whisper, "Company's coming," you can count on at least one of them to spark, fritz, and croak.

I'm not paranoid; I just happen to know that most major appliances are in cahoots. They seek revenge for a life void of long-term maintenance agreements and regular cleaning sessions. And it's not just my appliances. This is a worldwide conspiracy.

Last weekend we arrived at a friend's house for a dinner party to find our hostess looking a little flustered. The dimmer switch to the dining room light was suddenly on the blink. Her husband twirled the switch a few times and threatened it under his breath, but it still refused to cooperate. Like that was a surprise.

Ten minutes later, the hostess emerged from the kitchen and announced the oven had quit working. You didn't need work boots and a tool belt to smell a full-fledged appliance revolt in process. Five minutes later, she emerged to announce the oven was working again.

That's how ovens are. They toy with you. No outright explosion, no total shutdown, just a power surge now and again that throws off your timing, gives you flushed cheeks and heart palpitations.

These appliance breakdowns happen with such regularity that they have nearly lost the element of surprise. Planning a party for ten? Plan on the vacuum cord fraying and refusing to kick in two hours before guests arrive. Having a ladies get-together? The toilet that works fine for the family will suddenly refuse to drop the flapper down over the drain.

There's nothing our sadistic toilet likes better than hearing me instruct an acquaintance to "jiggle the handle."

Our washing machine waited to puddle all over the floor like a puppy until an old friend stopped by for coffee. The repairman dispatched to fix the problem said a seal had worn out. "Boy, you don't see this happen often," he said, shaking his head. You do if you have vengeful appliances.

The dishwasher, may it rest in peace, threw a hissy fit in the rinse cycle after a big Fourth of July cookout. We didn't hear a peep out of it the rest of the summer. Thanksgiving Day it upchugged and the heating element staged a complete meltdown. It was the first family holiday we'd had at our house in five years. A coincidence, you say? I don't think so.

You want conniving, take our rangehood exhaust fan over the stove. Worked like a charm until the day I made blackened chicken and a houseguest was napping upstairs. The instant I threw that chicken into the skillet and smoke started to billow, the fan sputtered to a stall. I was terrified our guest would wake up, see smoke, and jump out the upstairs window—which I suppose all of our maniacal appliances would have found highly entertaining.

Appliances are nothing to be afraid of. You just have to remind them who's boss. The next time I entertain, I'm strolling around the kitchen with a few sale circulars from appliance stores. Two can play this little game.

HINTS FROM HELL-OISE

QUICK! Name a homemaker's three best friends. Hint: They're that reliable trio that insure your survival through Little League season, plumbing disasters, and birthday parties for four-year-olds.

If you said Lunchables, a VISA card, and tokens for Chuckie Cheese Pizza, you have just revealed a serious and shameful lack of professionalism. Any woman, anywhere, remotely worthy of a self-defrosting refrigerator, should know a homemaker's three best friends are ammonia, white vinegar, and bleach.

Ignorant of the correct answer myself, I have unplugged my refrigerator, instructed the kids to load it onto the Radio Flyer, and roll it curbside for immediate pickup. This personal deficit crisis in homemaking skills was brought to my attention by the *All New Hints From Heloise: A Household Guide for the '90s*. Heloise is a Homemaker Hall of Famer who has earned a capital *H* on that title by drafting domestic platforms like "Getting a Hold on Mold," "Stuck on Non-Stick Pans," and "Stop That Spot."

I don't usually read time-saving household hint books. As a matter of fact, I lump them in the same category as bumper stickers that say "I love my schnauzer" and "Visualize World Peace"—interesting and no doubt life-changing to a sincere and passionate sector of the population, but not for me. So it was with mild curiosity that I passed a Heloise book at the library and cracked it open. It was out of shame that I became hooked on it.

Four hundred pages later, I now possess the confidence to wipe out any strained carrot, mustard, and blood stain, most airborne childhood viruses, and large reptile infestations, armed only with my utility belt containing vinegar, bleach, and ammonia.

Perhaps you'd like to test your own expertise at how to handle some sticky domestic situations:

If you get small slivers in your hand from steel wool, you should:

a. walk to a Dunkin' Donuts and see if you can find a couple of paramedics on break
b. carefully remove the slivers with sterilized barbecue tongs

c. let some Elmer's Glue dry on your hand and then pull
it off, taking the slivers with it

Heh, heh. That was a trick question, because paramedics
rarely break at Dunkin' Donuts—they eat at Burger King!
The correct answer, according to Heloise, would be "c."

If you drop a raw egg on a vinyl floor, you could:

a. wipe it up with a paper towel moistened with a 3:1
vinegar and water solution
b. call in a hungry dog
c. sprinkle salt on it and let it sit for 12 to 20 minutes

That's right, a real homemaker would heavily salt the
egg blob, ignite flares, reroute all indoor traffic around the
hazard zone, and then, twenty minutes later, sweep it up
with a broom.

Today's modern high chair should:

a. have an attached abacus so baby can begin learning
mathematics through manipulatives
b. be of a durable lightweight molded plastic that will
endure the spray from a pressure nozzle connected to a
fire hose
c. have a towel bar mounted to the side for easy cleanup,
nonskid daisies on the chair seat to anchor baby's bottom, and a plastic drop cloth underneath the chair to
catch baby's crumbs

Once again, the answer is "c." By following all of Heloise's
suggestions for a tidy and safe high chair, the final contrap-
tion will closely resemble a UFO.

A nifty way to clean a toilet bowl is to:

a. drop in denture tablets, let them foam, then brush and flush

b. pour in a flat cola and let it sit for an hour, then brush and flush

c. light two M-80s and quickly drop the lid

Both "a" and "b" were correct. (Note: "c" works too, as was demonstrated by members of my high school senior class, but also results in an unpleasant call from the Alcohol, Tobacco, and Firearms people.)

If you answered all the questions correctly, you are either the sneaky, competitive type who cheated, or you vacuum in the big league and probably even have pet names for your vacuum's attachments.

The inherent risk in converting to Heloisism is that of losing your objectivity on life. Empty margarine tubs, used sandwich bags, and old twist ties suddenly become objects of tremendous value and adoration. The next thing you know, you're cutting six one-inch slashes (like an asterisk) in a plastic lid, shoving your hair through and wearing it to back-to-school night as a ponytail holder. And really, after you've gone that far, what's left to do for fun?

UNFINISHED PROJECTS

Sure, you don't notice them as soon as you step into the house. They're fairly well camouflaged, but they're here. They're everywhere.

One lurks in a plastic bag tucked behind some old sheet music in the hall closet. It's three yards of cotton knit stamped with ocean blue seashells. I fully intended to sew both of the girls a sundress last summer, but then it seemed like they had enough clothes after all.

The bookshelf in the family room is loaded with them. There's the cake decorating book that was a gift. Someone thought I'd enjoy learning how to make those fancy frosting roses that adorn the pretty cakes in the bakery window.

Every one of my roses turned out looking like a pale pink igloo after a heat wave. Nestled next to the once-used cake decorating book is a manual on how to teach yourself Hebrew. I have a faint memory of being inspired by Oliver Wendell Holmes. He mastered twenty foreign languages in his lifetime and tackled Chinese at age eighty. I recall thinking, if an eighty-something guy could tackle Chinese, how hard could it be for a thirty-something gal to tackle Hebrew? Real hard.

On the shelf below rests the *Birds of North America* and the *Kids' Nature Book*. Once we mastered bird identification, I was positive a nature experiment a day would transform the kids into contemporary version of Henry David Thoreau and John James Audubon.

The kitchen is a virtual minefield. At least one crouches silently in the darkness of every other cabinet. Buried at the back of the utensil drawer is a melon-baller from a brief fling at sculpting watermelons into whales. Quietly waiting in the buffet is a half-embroidered holiday table runner. Shoved to the back of the hotpad drawer are four yellow candy molds. Theoretically, you were supposed to be able to make cream cheese mints in the shape of leaves and bells so lovely they would be suitable for a wedding. Mine had to be dug out of the molds with toothpicks.

The larger-scale doomed experiments have congregated in the garage. The great herb garden of '91 is now housed in several dozen Baggies. The herbs are so dried and brown that parsley looks like basil and oregano resembles marjoram. Or is it thyme?

Behind a motion detector light still in the box (the neighborhood crime wave ebbed) is a small box of rubber snakes, which I was sure would keep rabbits out of the herb garden. Next to the snakes sits a hardened half-empty gallon of Wild Raspberry paint from an attempt to make a bold color statement in the bathroom. It looked a lot bolder (terrifying is more accurate) on the wall than on the paint chip.

It's quite a collection of half-finished, half-baked projects. I could rout them all out in a robust round of spring cleaning and simply trash these reminders of things left undone. Or I could box them all up for the Goodwill or Salvation Army. (Then again, why punish the needy?)

I could put them in the garage sale and make a few bucks. (Then again, they'd probably just get taxed.)

Or maybe I just need to put them in a different light. Instead of regarding these skeletons in the closet as reminders of ideas and family projects that fizzled, instead of letting them induce guilt and anxiety, maybe they simply need to be relabeled. That's it, they need the help of a spin doctor.

Instead of "Stupid Ideas That Didn't Pan Out," they will now be known as "Possibilities Void of Further Potential." I think I can live with that.

But just in case, can I interest anyone in a slightly used candle dipping kit and a box of upholstery tacks?

MECHANICALLY CHALLENGED

The sign out front read: "Identifying the problem is half the solution." I must have believed it. How else could I rationalize walking down a flight of stairs in a strange building to meet with a group of people I'd never laid eyes on before?

The stairs led to a long meeting room with a linoleum floor that made the click of my heels sound angry. Metal folding chairs were arranged in a circle toward the far end of the room.

Sliding into the last empty seat, I sheepishly introduced myself. "Hi. I'm Lori, and I'm mechanically challenged."

Muttered welcomes resounded from the group. The guy next to me extended a hand. Even without the two fingertips he lost to a weed trimmer, he had a firm grasp.

The moderator was on crutches and in a full-leg cast. (Seems there'd been an unfortunate incident about a month back involving some guttering and a ladder.) He asked if anyone wanted to share. Nobody volunteered, so he went for it himself.

"Tough week," he said, hiking up his tool belt. "I heard a knocking on the outside of the house. Three pieces of roofing were flapping in the wind. The wife begged me to ignore it till I was on both legs again, but I couldn't let it go. I was in the garage, just about to pull the extension ladder off its hook with my crutch, when somehow, somewhere, I found the power to slowly back away."

The group exploded with applause.

As shouts of congratulations died down, a thirty-something woman began to speak. "It all began with WD-40. I could handle a can pretty well," she said. "I fixed the swing set, even took the squeak out of the baby's crib. Then I moved on to the hard-core stuff—home-repair books. I was only trying to save a little money. It started with the *Reader's Digest* series. But that wasn't enough. I needed one more, and just one more. *Better Homes and Garden*. The Bob Vila videotapes. I'm up to a $240-a-month habit and still can't do anything more complex than loosen a rusty bolt."

The kid spoke next. He couldn't have been older than fourteen, maybe fifteen, tops. "It's my d-d-dad," he stammered. "We've begged him to call a professional, but he refuses. He strips every screw hole and shorts every circuit he touches. We've been without a toilet in the upstairs bathroom since '94. It's always 'just one more trip to the hardware store,' and he's sure he'll have it."

Surprisingly, I heard myself speaking up. "I always believed there was a mechanic trapped inside me waiting to get out. Why not? I played with Tinkertoys as a child. I even come from a good gene pool for the mechanically gifted. But the only gene I inherited is Destructo Dominant. I just want to know one thing: Other people can handle power tools, copier machines, and assembly manuals with no problem. Why can't I?"

"Well," a wanna-be electrician with singed eyebrows said, "some just can, some can't. Live with it."

As the meeting drew to a close, group members clasped one another's scarred and bruised hands and recited the Prayer of Discretion for the Mechanically Challenged:

> *God grant me the serenity to accept the disasters I cannot fix, courage to fix the things I can, and wisdom to know when to call a professional.*

THE $64 TOMATO

Some people waste time; some people waste money. My husband and I have hit upon the best way to waste both. Obviously, I am referring to lawn maintenance.

Just last week I was reminded of how faithfully we excel at taking money out of our own pockets and planting it directly into the cash registers of lawn and garden stores. Last week is when we once again commenced the time-honored tradition of "The Patch."

This is how it works: We search out ugly spots in the lawn by blindfolding ourselves, spinning in a circle three times, and heaving a forty-pound bag of topsoil in any direction. Since our yard has more bare spots than grassy spots, wherever the bag lands is a fine place to begin working.

After using a rake to loosen soil in the bare spot, we scatter costly Kentucky bluegrass seed, cover it with loose topsoil, firmly tap the seed into place with the backside of the rake, and then pull up lawn chairs to watch the robins and cardinals begin to gorge themselves.

Of course, there is more than one way to effectively subsidize the grass seed, topsoil, and fertilizer industries. Another method is to coordinate lawn care efforts with the weather. To fully maximize wasted effort, you must wait for a two-hour window of sunshine followed by a fifteen-minute violent thunderstorm. That way, whatever grass seed the birds didn't snarf up, savage winds and torrents of water will wash into the gutters and flush down the sewer.

Few pleasures can exceed the joy and debt of lawn care, with perhaps the exception of cultivating your own Neiman-Marcus tomato.

Anybody can go to the grocery store and pick up a pack of vine-ripened tomatoes in a vacuum-sealed pack. Sure, they're red, they're round, and you don't have any dirt under your fingernails after you harvest them, but they're six for $2.99. Why not spend a little more time, just a little more effort, and wait till late August or early September for the satisfying taste of a homegrown $64 tomato?

Here's how it's done: Purchase six seedling tomato plants, fourteen feet of fencing, and wire cutters. This comes to $39.75 (the tetanus shot will run you an extra $65). Stick those Big Boys in the dirt, fence them in, and let them grow five days.

The following weekend, go out and buy rabbit repellent, slug bait, and six new tomato plants to replace the ones the critters destroyed. Cost: $25. Then, just to let those rabbits know you have a surveillance strategy firmly in mind, throw in a $199 hammock.

Taking pride in your produce, you'll also want to pick up some Wonder Grow, a patented Wonder Grow spray applicator, and tomato dust to fight mites, aphids, and bores, which will come to about $37. The increase in your water bill, the six-position sprinkler on a timer, and the combination Hand Cultivator and Mulcher as seen on the Home Shopping Network will run you around $90. Throw in a couple of tickets to a Reds baseball game (stress has its price) and you're looking at a cool half-a-grand invested in tomatoes.

Quit balking; either you like tomatoes or you don't. Besides, unit pricing will bring the cost down to a mere $64 a tomato. And can you really put a price tag on good flavor?

There's nothing as wonderful as a firm, ripe, home-grown tomato on a hot summer day. Well, there might be a few things, but at $64 a tomato, you sure can't afford to admit it.

DOWNSIZING HOUSEWORK

You may have noticed that while women were fighting for equal rights in the workplace, men were not marching on Washington waving dustpans and brooms, demanding an end to discrimination on the domestic front.

To my knowledge, not one man has filed suit in federal court for equal access to vacuums and sponge mops. Nor has one guy burned his boxers in protest because he was denied the opportunity to iron his shirts or defrost the freezer.

As a result of such lopsided liberation, it is frequently wives who pay a price when they attempt to pass the baton of household chores to their husbands. And may I just say— speaking as a liberated woman who chases three kids, runs a house, gets the oil changed in the car, maintains a marriage, occasionally mows the yard, and works part-time—any more liberation will probably outright kill me.

The fact is, whenever a mom is gone from home, for whatever reason, she always plays a quick round of catch-up when she returns. For some women, playing catch-up is as simple as wiping jelly off the doorknob. For others, it means making phone calls to drywall contractors.

I can't help but wonder what NASA astronaut Shannon Lucid encountered when she returned home after spending a record 188 days in space. Women pay for an absence like that.

Why? Because the average husband does about five to eight hours of indoor housework per week (a statistic some believe may have a four-hour margin of error—you guess which way), whereas the average wife still spends about twenty to thirty hours on these tasks.

Don't shrug it off, fellas. That housework adds up to a very pretty penny. A family practice attorney and a financial planner applied national-average wages to the average amounts of time women spend performing routine tasks. They found that a full-time homemaker, if paid for twenty-two different services (including waitress, chauffeur, house-keeper, bookkeeper, dishwasher, hostess, gardener, nanny, cook, dietitian, tutor, laundress, family counselor, child psychologist, and secretary), would rake in a whopping $108,048.73 annually.

What's that you say, ladies? Full- or part-time home-maker, you don't think you've been paid any such amount? I'll wait while you check your tax records. I thought so.

Not only have you been doing a considerable amount of work for free, without comp time or a three-day weekend over Presidents Day, you occasionally meet with resistance when you merely suggest a more equitable distribution of household chores.

What's a woman to do?

Downsize. That's right. Fire yourself. Give yourself a tidy little compensation package: spare change you can find under the sofa cushions, that last Fudgsicle you found hidden in the freezer, an Alaskan cruise. Whatever. The point is, you need to kick back and lay low for several days—or 188—whatever it takes for your family to miss your valuable multi-tasking domestic skills.

Then, when they make those really sad puppy eyes, give them all a hug and offer to contract out the majority of household work—to yourself—at current union pay scales.

Fine, so it probably won't work. But consider the layoff, at least for a day. It may not translate into hard cash, but who knows, you might gain something even better.

Appreciation.

GET THE (CHEEP) HOUSE OF YOUR DREAMS

I finally found the charming Midwestern farmhouse I've always dreamed of: a two-story white clapboard with a red brick chimney, brass weather vane, shuttered windows, and rambling front porch.

The location is equally as picturesque. It sits in a grove of towering sycamores, overlooking rolling hills and a winding stream. The really great part is, it is well within our budget. There's only one small problem—it was built for birds.

Birds are faring better than people these days when it comes to real estate. They're getting fantastic housing at affordable prices—Victorian gingerbread models, Southwestern-style haciendas, and Greek Revival mansions—all for under $49.95.

The most elaborate spread I've seen was a replica of Dodge City, Kansas, in the days of the Wild West. It was made of interlocking birdhouses, a saloon, boardinghouse, general store, telegraph office, and jail. They were so authentic that birds were spitting sunflower hulls on the saloon floor and heaving drunken insects through the swinging tavern doors and into the horse trough.

Those birdhouses we used to slap together as kids with chunks of cheap plywood are now the shanties of birdhouses. They're the run-down fixer-uppers that Habitat for Herons descends upon over a three-day weekend to gut, refinish, and refurbish.

Personally, I have to wonder if finches, blue jays, and sparrows truly appreciate all this customized housing. Sure, a few of your more flamboyant birds might value good design. Take barn swallows, the Frank Lloyd Wrights of bird circles. They build those futuristic oval houses out of mud paste and then dangle them precariously from beams in barns—not unlike the nuts in California who build sleek, multimillion-dollar houses on ocean overlooks.

But what about your average bird, your typical cardinal with an IQ of peat moss who will make a 75-mph kamikaze dive bomb at his own reflection in a car's sideview mirror? Does a bird like that have the intelligence to appreciate attention to architectural detail?

We've tried to lure birds with brains of any size by offering a variety of simple but stylish homes. We offer the Garden of Eden model shaped like a bright red apple, with an eat-in kitchen and walk-out sun deck. Two chickadees took a couple of walk-throughs, but turned up their snooty little beaks. We also had Haven-in-the-Alps, a cozy A-frame made of roofing shingles accented with adorable hand-painted scroll trim. For a time, it mildly interested several sparrows. Then, just to cover all the bases, we trucked in the Hillbilly Hootenanny, a lean-to made out of a rusted 1957 license plate.

Despite our wide range of offerings, not to mention the all-you-can-eat seed bar open twenty-four hours a day, convenient shopping, and good schools, we have had few takers. Oh, the birds stay. Just not in the houses.

A purple finch has built a nest and is presently sitting on five speckled eggs in a Boston fern. Two sparrows are frantically putting the finishing touches on a nest in a decrepit grapevine wreath hanging on the back door, and a family of robins has staked out a solid branch and begun home construction in a white pine.

Seems most of today's birds prefer the old traditional twig-and-stick housing under open skies and starry nights. Go figure—birds getting back to nature.

DOES NOT COMPUTE

Stress and computers go together like holidays and stomach flu. I view setting up a new computer as the nerve-racking, hair-pulling, nail-biting dose of personal trauma that the pay-per-call Customer Support Services intended it to be. Kids believe setting up a new computer is equivalent to a decade of birthdays, Christmas at Grandma's, and a trip to Disney World all rolled into one. Maybe they're right. They do cost about the same.

While I am still unfolding the picture poster instructions on how to remove the computer components from the box, the kids have it fully assembled, booted up, and are adjusting things like the RAM, cache, and virile memory. While I am refolding the picture poster instructions, they have set the sound panel to quack like a belligerent duck whenever someone (me) makes an error, and are listening to an audio CD through the computer while registering software via the phone.

I remind them that this "toy" is my office and that I would like to organize a few files before they commandeer it. Right. Like someone could actually "work" with miniature clones of Bill Gates breathing down your neck, shouting keyboard shortcuts, and grilling you as to why you won't let them route the modem through the toaster.

Undaunted, I position myself before the keyboard. After several foiled attempts to transfer data from the old computer to the new computer, I'm left with two nagging questions. Question No. 1: Why does the computer reject my neatly labeled disks containing work from the past three years, but it readily accepts a grubbed-out disk bearing an icon of a dragon and the title "Dave's Secret Stuff"? Question No. 2: Who is Dave?

I'm pretty sure Dave is one of the neighborhood kids standing behind me chuckling over the fact that I have a computer learning curve remarkably similar to toothpaste. Frustrated, I back away from the machine as the younger set crowds in and engages in lively discussion.

Naturally, it is easy to see how the kids would become animated over whether to open the compact disk encyclopedia, world almanac, or 3-D atlas first. But wait. This is not a minor disagreement—this is war. And these are not my children. They are full-fledged Mac-heads, now willing to eject and reformat each other's brains over which background color to make the monitor screen. We have spent hundreds and hundreds of dollars on a highly educational tool, and the premier crisis is whether the monitor background should be a blinding iridescent green or teddy bears holding hands.

Our old computer had a small seven-inch black-and-white monitor that produced a gray background screen. The new computer has a screen as large as our television and more colors and textures than you'd find at Francine's World of Fabrics.

It's like that everywhere you go on this computer. We have gone from a simple vanilla and chocolate computer to the land of thirty-one flavors. With each additional menu of increased choices, I sigh and wonder if I'll even master a portion of them. The kids see the expanded options and scream, "YES! More choices, more power!"

I find I'm best able to sort through these choices when the kids are out of the house. It's slow going, but after only six torturous days and sleepless nights, I am definitely making progress. I finally broke into Dave's Secret Stuff disk, figured out a game called Specter, and scored enough points to qualify as Top Gun.

MARTHA STEWART AND ME

There's no middle ground, mulched, composted, or freshly tilled, when it comes to Martha Stewart. People either love her or they hate her.

Me? I love Martha. Any woman who can identify seven critical steps to making a bed (I thought the only requirement was to get the warm bodies out first) deserves to be a national icon.

Personally, I like to think that Martha isn't all that different from myself. After all, she has two arms; I have two arms. She lives in a house; I live in a house. She has two full-time gardeners; I have . . . oh well, bad example.

We really do share a lot of similarities, and I can prove it if you will just turn to page eight of *Martha Stewart Living* magazine. Here you will see a copy of Martha's May calendar.

Believe me, I was as shocked as anybody to see how parallel Martha's life runs to mine. According to the calendar, on May 1 Martha scheduled her pool maintenance. This is uncanny, but on May 1, I was in my garage standing in the kids' Red Flyer wagon, wedged between two trash cans, looking for sandpaper in the cabinet above the workbench, when I came across a little swatch of plastic and a tube of goo, which I instantly recognized as the patch kit to our flexible kiddie pool. Granted, Martha's pool is in-ground and probably lined with hand-painted ceramic tiles from Italy, and mine is the $14.95 job from SuperMart, but the point is, we were both thinking about pools on the same day.

81

In the second week of May, Martha plans on checking her outdoor hoses. I did that just this weekend. I was watering some weeds in the yard and saw a magnificent rainbow in front of me. The rainbow had been spawned by a geyser that had erupted in the garden hose. Martha and I do part company here. She will buy new hoses, while I will fix mine with a roll of duct tape, which, come to think, I've never seen used on her show. (Make a note: Send Martha an idea for a show on duct tape.)

Martha is having her air conditioner units serviced in May. I am taking care of mine, too. Every time I walk by it, I pray it will last one more year.

Martha has a lot of speaking engagements on tap for the month of May. I do a lot of speaking as well, the only difference being that most of mine is to an audience of three trapped in the kitchen, the car, or around the dinner table. Martha's speaking will have her before large groups in Toronto and Salt Lake City. I've heard murmuring behind my back that I would be welcome to take my speaking out of town, but to date, the farthest I've let them push me is the backyard.

Of course, Martha and I don't do everything alike. She plans on moving tomato, pepper, and eggplant seedlings into the vegetable garden this month. I plan on moving tomato, pepper, and eggplant from the produce shelf to plastic bags to the checker. She'll judge live poultry in Bloomsburg, Pennsylvania; I'll judge thawed poultry at the stove, wondering if two days past the expiration date runs a serious risk of salmonella.

My schedule and Martha's may differ on some of the finer details but, when it comes to the big picture, she and I are kindred spirits. After all, it's not just a coincidence that both of our May calendars are rectangular-shaped, have thirty-one days, and run from Sunday through Saturday.

It's a good thing.

6

For Better or for WORSE

My husband is a collector who loves to save stuff. My motto is "Heave, Ho!" I love to pitch anything left lying in the same spot more than two days. This is not the only difference we somehow failed to notice before we married.

He's a night owl; I'm a morning person. He loves the sun; I burn like a lobster. I like to be spontaneous; he can't leave the house without a thirty-minute security ritual. I figure a story isn't worth telling unless I can stretch it six ways till Sunday. He's a stickler for chronological order, accuracy, and details.

We were strangely blind to all these differences as we pledged to love each other until death do us part. All we could see were the myriad of things we had in common. Similar interests may have fanned the flames originally, but it is our quirky differences that keep the sparks flying and the embers hot.

WEDDING VOWS: TAKE TWO

I thought it strange when my husband asked what I thought about renewing vowels.

"I think I'll just stick with *a, e, i, o, u,* and sometimes *y,*" I said.

"*Not vowels,*" he said, "*vows*—marriage vows."

Ooooooooh, vows. "I don't think it's a good idea for us," I said.

"Why not?"

"Because we know all kinds of stuff about each other now that we didn't know years ago."

"You're saying you wouldn't renew?" he asked.

"No, I would renew. I would just want to insert some clarifications, a little leverage, and a few stipulations," I said.

"Like what?"

"You know that part about 'Do you take this man in sickness and in health?'"

"Sure," he said.

"Well, I'd find it a lot easier to promise to love you in sickness and in health if you would promise not to sprawl on the couch for two days moaning and groaning, but refuse to take an aspirin because you're not sure it will help. It also would be a perfect time to disclose those preexisting conditions you brought to the marriage."

"What preexisting conditions?" he asked.

"Conditions like your pack rat syndrome, that deep-seated fear of vacuuming, and chronic bouts of wife-deafness," I said. "While we're at it, that 'for better or for worse' part could use a little clarification, too."

"How's that?" he said, looking a little ashen.

"I'd promise to curb a few of my mood swings if you'd promise to quit ripping articles from newspapers in bed when I'm trying to go to sleep. Up your ante with a pledge to cut that home security ritual you go through every time we leave

84

town (timers, lamps, radio, miniblinds, porch lights) to twenty minutes and I think you'd be holding a pretty good hand."

"You make marriage sound like a poker game," he said.

"There's not a high roller out there who wouldn't agree it's a sizable gamble," I retorted. "I'm just trying to put a little honesty into all of this.

"Speaking of which," I said, " 'for richer or poorer' could use a reality check. Everybody assumes that the happy couple will ride off into the sunset and hit pay dirt. We should just promise to take turns racing deposits to the bank in hopes of beating the checks."

"So, you're saying if you had it to do over again, you would still choose to marry that same good-looking hunk of burning love [Note to the reader: He means himself.] you first met twenty years ago?" he asked.

"No," I said. "I can't renew vows with that young pup. He doesn't exist anymore. The person I was doesn't exist either. How could we?

"Over the years we've been through one duplex, two houses (one infested with termites, the other held hostage by carpenter ants), job changes, a cross-country move, a miscarriage, the birth of three children, the death of a parent, and one car accident. We've both lost hair, patience, and tempers and added glasses, weight, and a lot of wrinkles. I can't renew vows with that young greenhorn, but I could renew them with you."

"You really think you would?" he asked.

"I do."

BUNDLES OF FUN

Some men feel secure only when they have a beer can in their hands. For others it is a remote control or a golf club that does the trick. Not my husband. For him, security is a newspaper.

On the one hand, security truly is a newspaper because we both work for them. On the other hand, he takes them far more seriously than I do. I read a newspaper by shaking sections apart, creasing pages in thirds, ripping out interesting articles, and then wrapping melon rinds and chicken bones in whatever's left. He reads a newspaper by slowly opening each section, neatly folding each page, putting the sections back in order, and then taking it to one of his thirty-seven collection sites. He operates on a "more the merrier" philosophy, believing a man can never save too many newspapers.

We have a collection the Smithsonian would envy. From Missouri to Minnesota to Oregon, every last newspaper either one of us has ever worked for is somewhere in this house. (He will tell you that's a lie, but he's not writing this story, I am.)

If you'd like the answers to a crossword puzzle that ran in 1976, give me a call. I'm sure we have it. Want to know what kind of advice Ann Landers was dispensing to cross-dressers in 1982? No problem. I'm sure we can find it in the garage somewhere. Or the attic. Or the upstairs closet.

The collection ritual goes like this: My husband's initial collection site is the kitchen counter. Newspapers linger there until I give him one of those meltdown stares that says, "Do something about those or I'll do something about those for you." He then gathers up the papers and proceeds to the intermediate level of the archival process—piling them on a kitchen chair.

Two weeks later, he will shuffle the newspapers again and take them to a designated stacking area that I have strict instructions not to disturb. There are enough newspapers that we could build a six-foot flood wall around the house and still have enough left over to insulate the attic.

On occasion I have attempted to calmly step in and run an intervention. Last week I beat him to the stack of newspapers on the chair, gathered them up, and was spotted heading toward the back door.

"Where are you going with those?" he asked, peering over the top of the sports section.

"To the humane society. They called to say they were out of liners for the dog cages."

"You're lying," he said, "you're headed to the trash."

"You caught me. I was lying," I confessed. "I'm not going to the humane society. I'm going over to Diana's house. We're going to fold paper hats for children in Bosnia."

"That's not funny," he snapped with a glare.

From the look on his face, you'd think I was attempting to throw away a perfectly good side of beef. The way he carries on, you'd think these were diamonds, emeralds, and rubies I had in my arms instead of a stack of cheap, dry, brittle newsprint.

"Listen, sweetheart," I said in my most soothing there's-no-need-to-work-yourself-into-a-tizzy voice, "I'm not going to the trash, but I am going outside for a little bit."

"What are you up to?" he asked.

"Nothing, really. Just relax. And whatever you do, don't panic if you see smoke."

A TALE OF TWO STORMS

Surviving a tornado was definitely the highlight of our summer vacation. I'm telling you, it was a near-Oz experience.

My husband will tell you that we survived nothing more than a severe thunderstorm. Same hot and humid afternoon, same spot at the side of a two-lane highway—vastly different interpretations.

It was like Siskel and Ebert reviewing the same movie. One says thumbs-up and the other says thumbs-down. It was like two people witnessing the same traffic accident. One eyewitness insists the truck ran the red light while another witness swears the light was still green long after the truck cleared the intersection.

I have often wondered how two people can witness the same event, yet come away with completely different versions of what happened. Now I know. One of them is nuts.

The storm I witnessed began building shortly after three in the afternoon when lightning bolts struck at the ground with relentless brutality. Towering thunderheads rapidly changed from sweatsuit gray to a dark charcoal. Lower layers of clouds broke off and spun like sugar being whipped into cotton candy. Ditto for my husband. He didn't spin like cotton candy—he witnessed the changing sky, too.

The storm I observed unleashed its terrible fury seconds after blinding rain forced us to pull to the side of the road. Ditto for my husband.

Here is where our observations and storms part paths. I recall the van shaking and rocking wildly, trees bending to the ground, and baseball-size hail being imminent. By my husband's account, the van was stationary and trees were merely swaying. The reason he accidentally hit the button that opened the van's rear gate instead of the one that turns on the flashers is vague—but it certainly wasn't because he panicked or because the van was bouncing up and down like it was parked on a trampoline.

I maintain the aftermath of the storm is concrete proof we were in a tornado. Only a few yards down the road, a huge barn was flattened like a miniature paper parasol that had suffered two months in the bottom of my purse after being salvaged from a tropical drink. I also saw a six-foot plank driven straight through the center of a tree.

In the storm aftermath my husband witnessed, the barn was merely collapsed on one side, not dramatically flattened. The plank was not a plank but only an eighteen-inch segment of two-by-four. Nor was it driven through the tree, but gently resting between a natural fork of the branches.

What we have here is a difference in perception. You have one mind relying heavily on a barometric pressure gauge, humidity percentages, wind direction, colored felt tip pens, and certified meteorologists. In contrast, you have another mind that paints with a broad brush, relies largely on sensory input, a high caffeine intake, and big band music heavy on the bass.

Let the record show that I witnessed a tornado while my husband witnessed a severe thunderstorm, straight line winds, microburst, or some other highfalutin term they bounce around on the Weather Channel. Until his dying day he will insist it couldn't possibly have been a bona fide tornado for two logical reasons: He sighted neither a funnel cloud nor the sky turning an eerie shade of green.

Fine. I suppose he didn't see Toto bounce off the front windshield or the pair of ruby red slippers fly past either.

HONEY CAN'T FIND THE MUSTARD

The theory is that long, long ago, when men wore beards and the women were nearly as hairy, too, females gathered nuts and berries and tended the home and hearth, while menfolk ventured into the wilds perfecting their roles as hunters.

Traditionally, hunting has long been recognized as the superior skill embodied by the male gender. But if this is so, could someone please explain why three out of four men are unable to find the green pepper sitting in their refrigerator, let alone hunt down a birthday card for their own mother?

The hunter theory is bunk. My own personal hunter recently announced that we were out of mustard. Not true, I said, there is some on the pantry shelf in the garage.

My hunter disappeared for thirty seconds...sixty seconds...a minute and a half. He returned from the hunt empty-handed.

"It's not there," he said.

"Yes it is," I countered.

"Then I can't find it."

Can't find it? How hard did he hunt? We're not talking about tracking a wild turkey darting in and out of thick underbrush in three square miles of untamed wilderness. We're talking about hunting down a bright yellow container on a shelf unit that is half the size of Dr. Ruth.

I accompany my hunter to the garage and immediately shield my eyes with my hands to protect them from the brilliant glow of yellow radiating from behind a bottle of ketchup. Surprise! Mustard. Second shelf.

Could it be that the male hunting skills are selectively applied? Hunting skills are keen on the golf course, where they are effortlessly able to spot a ball the size of a black walnut five hundred yards away. Yet ask that same eagle eye to find a pound of margarine in the freezer and he looks at you like a sad puppy who knows he's about to be whacked on the nose with a rolled-up newspaper for leaving a small puddle in the hallway.

Why does an accountant, who successfully hunts and tracks teeny, tiny decimal points buried deep within stacks of computer printouts all day, have to ask for help finding the box of trash bags on a six-by-two-foot workbench?

A man is able to hunt down four open seats at a crowded ballpark, smoothly maneuvering his way through a moving, throbbing, screaming mass of humanity—but at the drugstore he cannot find his wife's style and size of pantyhose on a stationary display rack.

Then there's the dad dispatched to the grocery store for a can of french fried onion rings critical to completing a green bean casserole. He returns with two free newspapers, a pack of lemon sugar cookies, and a little brown plastic spigot known as the "whale" that can be attached to a bathroom sink faucet, converting it into a drinking fountain. With minimal hunting effort, he is able to gather an armload of freebies, junk food, and trinkets—but no onion rings.

They must have been hiding them, he says. Sure, that's how all major grocery chains stay in business. They hide the products from the shoppers.

My theory is that the male hunting skills still exist, they just diminish in strength the closer they get to hearth and home.

WE DO TAXES

We have been feverishly working on completing our tax return. When I say "we," I mean my husband and myself. Naturally, I am using "we" in the figurative sense like my husband does when he says, "We ought to have Christmas at our house this year," and then disappears until January 15. I am using "we" the way my husband does when he says, "We ought to get that button sewn back on my navy jacket," or "we ought to make sour cream chicken enchiladas because we haven't had those in a very long time."

Long ago, I used to wonder if he had a mouse in his pocket when he would issue proclamations about what "we" ought to do. I eventually realized he had no silent partner, and his use of the word "we" was simply an age-old congenial way in which husbands subtly attempt to direct their wives.

Not a quick study, but considerably sharper than a box of rocks, I, too, have become adept at representational use of the pronoun "we." Hence, "we" are now doing the taxes.

Right after "we" finish the taxes, "we" are going to buy a gallon of paint and spruce up one of the kid's bedrooms. Right after that, "we" are going to clean up the workbench in the garage, and then "we" will replace a thermometer outside the kitchen window that has been off 17 degrees since last November.

But for now, "we" are pounding on the calculator and sweating bullets over a dozen or so tax forms. The specific division of duties between "we" goes like this: He organizes the financial records, double-checks the withholdings, itemizes interest, dividends, and contributions, and emits deep, old-man sighs at regular intervals. I stand around looking concerned and offer creative suggestions as to how "we" might be able to keep more of our own hard-earned money and still have the freedom to live at home, as opposed to behind bars in a federal penitentiary.

He does not think "we" should use creative-thinking strategies when dealing with the IRS. He does not think "we" are working well as a team.

At this point, as I traditionally do every year, I turn to the Tele-Tax listings in the 1040 Forms and Instructions booklet provided strictly for the taxpayers' entertainment and side-splitting laughter.

I begin with the tape on business entertainment deductions. How comforting to hear that it is perfectly legal to deduct the cost of entertaining clients at nightclubs, Wayne Newton concerts, NHL hockey games, hunting and fishing boondoggles, and Caribbean vacations.

It is also reassuring to know that line 6 of the 1040 is still limited to 50 percent of Schedule C, Part IV, line 15, (Attach form 8876), subtracted from line 2, and multiplied by the relative humidity before being adjusted to 2 percent of the gross income.

I pass along bits and pieces of information, which I believe would be helpful in completing our tax return, and am told that "we" are not amused.

It is then suggested that if one of us does not cease and desist from assorted distractions, a serious error could be committed. "We" could then be audited and "we" could go to jail.

Naturally, I must assume he is again using "we" in the figurative sense.

I'll miss him.

THERMOSTAT TAG

The annual Battle for the Thermostat officially kicked off last Wednesday night.

My husband jacked that baby up so high that all the houseplants croaked. Even the African violet. Right now it's so hot in here the tea kettle can go from zero to whistling in under ten seconds.

The man is a utility company's dream come true. The mercury dips below 72 and he fires up the furnace. For the next seven months we will be playing Thermostat Tag.

In the interest of good health, I begin the game by setting the thermostat at a comfortable 66 degrees.

"It's so cold in here you can see your breath," he complains a few minutes later.

"Yeah, isn't it great?"

The minute my back is turned, he darts to the thermostat and cranks it up to an unseasonable 74.

I ask, "What's the point in owning sweaters if I'm too hot to wear them?"

No answer.

Ten minutes later, I make a play for pity. I announce that I'm so hot, I'm gonna be sick.

A family of five and not one person responds.

I say, "I'm so hot, I think I'm gonna faint."

Again, no response.

I say, "I'm so hot, I'm gonna start peeling off my clothes."

My teenage son knocks over two chairs and the kitchen table lunging to his feet screaming, "No, no, don't do it! Don't do it! We'll turn down the temperature."

That's more like it.

Ten minutes later my husband is doing this fake shivering thing and two of the kids are walking around with blankets over their shoulders. They are all claiming that if we don't turn up the heat, everyone is going to catch a cold.

I say, "Better to build a little immunity now before the holidays hit."

The phone rings and it's my mother. She wants to know whether they'll need light jackets or heavy coats when they come for Thanksgiving.

"But, Ma, we're not eating outside."

"I know, dear. Your father and I were just wondering how cold you're keeping the house these days."

Everybody's a comedian.

I hang up the phone knowing full well that Mr. "I Love the Tropics" has been the last to hit the thermostat. I head upstairs before it's too late.

"Stay away from those vents," he hollers after me. "Did you hear me?"

Oh, I heard something, but it's hard to say exactly what when a guy is yelling through two scarves and a muffler.

"Fine," I yell back, "I won't close the upstairs vents."

I do, however, open our bedroom window and pull the blind down in front of it. I'll need some cool air in order to sleep, especially after being half-sick with heat exhaustion all day.

He comes to bed, senses a chill in the air, and makes some lame excuse about going downstairs to check the door.

He returns and I suddenly remember that I forgot to grind up the carrot peels in the garbage disposal. I beeline to the thermostat, which he has set to a sizzling 74. I don't touch the setting. I merely flip the teeny, tiny red power switch beneath it.

The next morning I see him dragging his foot across the hardwood floor by the window.

"Something wrong?" I ask.

"The floor is stone cold from this window someone opened." He looks at me intently and says, "You know the furnace is on."

"That's what you think," I say. "You're it."

ROMANTIC EBBS AND FLOWS

I fell in love with my husband again. It was Tuesday, 4:43 A.M. Not that I ever fell out of love with him, mind you, but within the heartbeat of marriage, there runs a secondary pulse of romantic ebbs and flows. It's the little things that throw me into a deep freeze or fan the flames of infatuation.

This one began when I was jarred awake shortly before five by the cries of a child trapped in a nightmare. Or so I thought. I checked the childrens' rooms and found they were snoozing soundly.

The cries grew louder. They came from beneath maple trees clustered in the backyard of the tidy ranch-style house across the street. They were the screams of a woman.

"No, Rocky, no! Stop, stop! Let go! Let go!" A barking dog added to the commotion.

I woke my husband. We listened from the bathroom window briefly while the terrified cries intensified.

"No, ROCKY! STOP! LET GO! LET GO!

"NOOOOOOOOOOOO!"

Dead silence.

My husband and I exchanged glances and briefly pondered the wisdom of meddling with anyone named Rocky. We don't know these neighbors well, but we know neither of them is named Rocky. Actually, the only Rocky either of us has known was played by Sylvester Stallone.

Who was Rocky? A burly 350-pound long-distance trucker scorned by love now seeking revenge? A previously docile friend of the family who thought the early morning hours would be a good time to unveil his split personality? In any case, I pictured our neighbor sprawled helpless on the ground (imagination in terror has always been a strong suit of mine; it's from my mother's side) drifting in and out of consciousness.

But just in case she *could* get up, I dashed to the phone. Six rings, no answer. Meanwhile my husband had pulled on his jeans and headed out the front door. As he stepped off the curb I thought maybe I should grab a bat, or cast-iron skillet, and follow him. Maybe I should get 911 on the line. Maybe we should have taken out that term life insurance policy. Maybe I'd just stay put and watch from the porch.

My husband boldly peered over the neighbor's privacy fence and asked if everything was okay, only to find the mister and missus surveying the crime scene. Rocky had attacked all right. But Rocky had a lot more in common with Charlie Brown's Snoopy than Sylvester Stallone.

Clearly not accustomed to receiving callers in their sleepwear, the neighbors mumbled a few words and everyone went their way.

Turns out the missus had heard Rocky barking and went outside to inspect. Rocky had engaged in combat with a feisty raccoon returning home from a night on the neighborhood garbage run. Not having a stomach for savagery, she began screaming at Rocky to let go of the raccoon.

Of course we didn't know any of those finer details when we became entangled in this predawn saga of passion and violence. Sure, it might be easier to subdue Rocky the pooch than Rocky with a mean left. But the point is, my better half was willing to face the unknown.

And as of 5 A.M. Tuesday I was not only reminded of those strengths that first made me love him, but that it might also be smart to learn the names of our neighbors' dogs.

THE LONG GOOD-BYE

His shock of white hair is combed straight back, his hazel eyes dance, and his hands gesture rapidly as he tells another tale. His memory is tack-sharp and packed full. It houses nearly eighty-six years of historical tidbits, important dates, and record-breaking temperatures.

She has celebrated eighty-five birthdays. She has snow-white hair, brown eyes that used to twinkle with mischief, and a memory that has been steadily failing for well on three years.

Plates are cleared from the table, and while all about agree the meal was fine, for some reason it has brought to his mind the death of President Warren G. Harding. He recalls that Harding traveled to the West Coast in 1923, dined in a swanky San Francisco hotel, and died several days later of food poisoning on August 2.

She is sitting at the table, oblivious to the story about Harding. She reaches for a paper napkin, holds it, examines it closely, turns it over, unfolds it, and slowly quarters it back into a square. "Would someone please tell me what this is?"

"Napkin," he says. "It is a paper napkin."

He then returns to remembering, because remembering the past sometimes makes it easier to forget the present.

He is now remembering a trip to Niagara Falls over Labor Day weekend in 1929. Round-trip fare from Dayton, Ohio, was about $7.50. He and two friends went downtown on Saturday evening, August 31, and walked around awhile before going to the depot to get on the train that left at 11 P.M.

"What is this?" she once again demands to know.

"A napkin, a paper napkin," he answers and returns to his story.

The train was pulled by a steam locomotive, fire tender attached next, and then a boxcar followed by about four or five coaches. He is debating whether they were in the last car or next to last car when she has another question.

Of the hundreds and hundreds of questions she asks in a day, "What is that? Where did that come from? What is that? Where did that come from?" this is the one that wrenches the heart.

"Who am I?" she asks in an agitated voice quavering with fear.

Who are you?

You are Oma, wife of this fellow with the stories and memory that never quit. You are the tomboy who roller-skated to school as a little girl and learned to dog-paddle in Bear Creek by watching your dog Buster. You are the dry wit and sharp mind that entered nurse's training at age eighteen. You are the rebel who defied your family's wishes and enlisted in the Army Nurse Corps, serving in the European theater during World War II.

Who are you?

You are the softie who never turned away a stray kitten and right now have eleven little toy dogs sitting on top of your television. You are a loyal Reds fan, a prayer warrior, and strong woman of deep faith. You are a patriot who loves the Fourth of July, Roman candles, and Whitney Houston singing the "Star Spangled Banner."

You are the party gal who danced the polka at my wedding. You are the mother of my husband, grandmother to my children, and my very dear friend.

You are a woman stricken by a disease that affects some six million Americans. It attacks the brain, corroding the memory and garbling thought.

There are ways to stall this disease, but there is no cure. It always ends in death. The disease is officially known as Alzheimer's. But to those who must watch it slowly steal precious bits and pieces of the ones they love, it could best be described as the Long Good-bye.

7

The HEART of Things

My mom's mental health used to worry me when I was growing up. It was the crazy things she said.

She'd say nutty things like, "Don't look at me that way. Look at me when I'm talking to you!" Or, "If you think I don't mean it, just try me." Now, *was* that an invitation or was that an invitation? One of my favorites was, "Did you think that would make me happy?" Talk about a loaded question. If I said, "Yeah, Ma, I thought that would make you happy," I was in big trouble. If I said, "No, Ma, I didn't think that would make you happy," I was in big trouble.

The all-time classic had to be, "This is going to hurt me more than it hurts you." That was a tough one to figure out, because she sure wasn't the one sitting home from a party Friday night.

I'm sure it's pretty obvious to you, my mom was a nut.

You want to know what the really scary part is? I'm becoming just like her.

WORK IS NOT OPTIONAL

To the best of my recollection, the discussion between my kid and me went something like this:

"But the teacher said extra credit work is optional," said my kid.

"She's wrong," said I.

End of discussion.

As my kid jerked the textbook off the table and walked away with a hangdog look, I momentarily wondered if I'm wrecking my kids the same way my parents ruined me.

My parents never let me think that going the full distance was optional either. They were from that Great Depression and World War II generation that believed you worked whether you felt like it or not. Work in any shape or form was never optional.

I'm guessing that since my parents never had a lot of options, they never gave us kids many either. Oh, it's not like we never had any freedom to choose. We always got to choose after a storm whether we wanted to help them pick up weeping willow branches from the backyard, or if we wanted to mouth off and pick them up by ourselves.

As I recall, my folks started eliminating our options first thing in the morning. They required that our beds were made and our rooms tidy before leaving for school. They never nagged about it, they just expected it. They always were a few laps behind the experts. They didn't buy the notion that kids should have the option of keeping their bedrooms in any condition they liked.

Nor did they ever allow us the option of snuggling deep into our beds when we thought we didn't feel well enough for school. Our only option was to get up, shower, get dressed, have breakfast, and then see how we felt. By the time we'd gone to that much trouble, we usually shuffled off to school.

We were free to choose butter or sour cream on baked potatoes. We were not allowed to choose whether we wanted fruits and vegetables. Those were not optional. Nor was sitting down to eat, clearing the table, and doing the dishes afterward.

Lounging at home on our duffs during the summer when we were old enough to work? Not an option. Nor was showing up late for a job ever optional.

Forgetting to put tools back where you found them? Not an option.

Not picking up jackets, shirts, or sweaters off the floor? It was an option tainted with danger. Those articles of clothing had a mysterious way of disappearing for several weeks and then reappearing in a box in the garage.

Talking back? A high-risk option.

Not following the rules? Naturally, as kids, we exercised that option from time to time, but we always knew we'd pay the price eventually.

When they did find that pack of cigarettes, or got a call from the school, they weren't real big on a lot of talk, exploring our feelings, and discussing our self-esteem. Debate never held the attraction for them that swift action did.

Of course, times are different today. We have scores of options that didn't exist thirty years ago. For every personal failure, discouragement, or hangnail, we have the option of blaming our parents, our gene pools, and our first-grade teachers who neglected to put a smiley face on our finger paintings. We have the option of pointing an accusing finger at our hormones, low self-esteem, the stress of technology, and corruptive influence of television.

Too bad I was so far into adulthood before discovering that the hard stuff like personal responsibility is as optional as a pocket handkerchief or hollandaise on asparagus. It's too late for me. I've already been brainwashed. What's more, here I am attempting to do the same thing to my kids.

I can only hope that some day they'll exercise the option to understand that I couldn't help it—I was victimized by an ancient malady fondly remembered as the work ethic.

WATCH YOUR WALLET

Buckle up for this news flash: Studies find kids are 80 percent more likely to wear seat belts when they see adults wear seat belts.

Imagine that. Kids imitating their parents. Who'da-thunkit?

Little people copying big people. Go figure.

It is one of those age-old truths that always manages to take us by surprise. It's an elementary concept cross-filed in our brains under *P* for parenting and *N* for no-brainer. Yet somehow, it never ceases to elicit a grin or a nod when we see it played out in real life.

Take the family where the mom and dad always finish off a meal by gnawing on a toothpick. Guess what their eight-year-old daughter routinely dangles from her mouth after dinner?

Take the young family that just welcomed a second child into their home. While mom changes the infant's diaper, the toddler swipes a dishtowel and tries to strap it to kitty's hindquarters.

You see it happen in front yards as a father pushes a deafening self-propelled lawn mower. Fifteen feet behind him a little boy follows in hot pursuit, pushing a bright orange plastic knock-off of the real thing.

The most vivid instance of seeing my behavior mirrored by a child happened a few years ago when our youngest bought a new wallet. She took the wallet to Grandma's house, whipped it out, and began displaying its many fine features.

She proudly displayed her new identification card, pictures of her school chums tucked into the plastic sleeves, and fifty-nine cents change in the coin compartment. She opened the fold where she would keep paper money, if she had any, and promptly began displaying cash register receipts.

She had a receipt from CVS for Jolly Ranchers, a receipt from where the two of us had lunch together three months prior, and an eighteen-inch-long receipt from Wal-Mart for toilet paper, shampoo, toothpaste, laundry soap, lightbulbs, glass cleaner, and other necessities. She had receipts from clothing stores, hardware stores, fast food joints, video stores, and the post office.

I looked at my child and thought what any mother would think: This kid is nuts. Why in the world would she save a huge wad of receipts in her wallet?

Then it hit me like a fully loaded grocery cart on the back of my heels. She saved receipts because I save receipts. Routinely, after purchasing any item that has a likelihood of self-destructing or not living up to the warranty, I tuck the receipt into my wallet.

Here's the real killer. I had never once told her to save receipts. I had instructed her to brush her teeth and hang up her clothes. I had nagged her about capitalizing proper nouns and riding her bike on the right side of the street, but not once had I hounded her to save receipts. Not a word spoken. I had never told her, but I had taught her.

Like the seat belt news flash, the wallet was a good reminder that kids may not be wearing trench coats and dark glasses, but they have adults under surveillance around the clock. They watch everything we do from the checkout aisle to the front seat of the car.

I knew that. You knew that, too. But when you're under scrutiny this intense, it doesn't hurt to be reminded.

ARE WE RICH?

"Are we rich or poor?" a voice from the backseat demanded to know.

That's not an easy question to answer, especially when you consider how children define wealth. Our youngest child regards anyone without a dog or a basement as "poor": We have neither, which accounts for the pitiful tone in which the question was asked. All three of the kids suspect anyone who drives a convertible or wears a lot of gold jewelry and leather is "rich."

"Super rich" is the woman they spotted at the grocery store a few years back. They didn't notice her ragged winter coat and summer sandals; all they could see was her cart overflowing with Choco-Tarts, Sugar Os, and corn dogs. They raced up and down the aisles to grab second and third peeks at such tremendous wealth. She paid with food stamps.

Shortly after that incident, we drove by a house with a two-car garage bursting with boxes, bags, and piles of stuff stacked to the ceiling. It was a scavenger's paradise and a firefighter's nightmare. One of the kids marveled out loud, "Wow! Wouldn't we be lucky to be that rich?"

To a young child, volume and quantity translate into rich.

To an older child, brand names and electronics equal wealth. Rich people are the ones wearing Michael Jordan's brand of basketball shoes while playing the latest Sega game connected to a wall-sized television screen.

Like many parents, we often pass on the pricey name-brand goods and substitute with lectures about money not growing on trees, the danger of living on credit, and the shame of bankruptcy. The kids thank us all the time.

We tell them we are postponing some of the bigger-ticket items until the day our ship comes in. They are skeptical as to whether our ship will ever come in. After all, they can't even see it on the horizon. (Fair point.) They believe it exists, mind you; they even think it has a name—the Titanic. (Cheap shot.)

I don't remember asking whether we were rich or poor as a young child. Maybe that's because we hadn't been baptized into a lifestyle of consumption. The home shopping network meant borrowing the neighbor's Sears catalog. The twenty-four-hour Deli and Dry-Goods Mega-Marts had yet to open their automatic doors.

So, are we rich or are we poor?

Well, we have reliable transportation and a comfortable house with indoor plumbing and a working furnace. We have bodies that work reasonably well, feet that faithfully carry us to the kitchen table, and ears that can hear the rustle of a potato chip bag two rooms away. We have eyes that can soak in the horror of the Mastercard bill and the glory of the Milky Way.

We live in a country free from the destruction of massive bombing and the terror of anarchy. We enjoy the right to speak without censorship, the freedom to worship in the way we choose and to gather with whom we please.

True, we experience setbacks and disappointments, illnesses and the sorrow of parting that accompanies death. But we also have access to God, who does not abandon us in despair or leave us without comfort.

We have family and friends (and we're thinking about a dog).

Are we rich?

Let's just say Donald Trump has nothing on us. We're rich, all right, wonderfully, blessedly rich.

DOWN IN THE POLLS

I'm not popular at home today.

It seems like only yesterday I was everybody's favorite partner for Crazy 8s, heralded as the World's Best Mom in a homemade card, and highly esteemed as the Champion Thumb Wrestler.

Now I'm on the out list. I'm yesterday's most beloved. Line me up behind Michael Jackson's sequined glove, polyester leisure suits, and Hillary's headbands.

My ratings have dipped to a five-week low. Confidence in my ability to perform my job has plummeted. These kids think I'm a vixen, the original dragon lady, the cruelest woman free from the confines of prison bars.

Oh, they wouldn't dare say it—well, two of them wouldn't, anyway. They mumble, murmur, and whisper about my personality disorder from around corners and behind closed doors. They're too calculating to say everything they think out loud.

Nonetheless, it is obvious from three sets of sullen eyes and set jaws that they firmly believe I've crossed the line from benevolent dictator to ruthless tyrant.

How did I earn this scorn, and incur such wrath?

I said no.

I said no, you can't call a friend until you help make dinner. I said no, because the fact is, I am not the Little Red Hen, who will plant the wheat, grind the wheat, and knead the dough all by myself, and then allow my little chicks to scurry gleefully to the table after the bread has been baked, sliced, and buttered.

I said no, you can't play on the computer until you finish that book report. I said no because your most important job as a child is school. Please, think of it as a career, and every one of you should feel free to turn yourselves into workaholics.

I said no, you can't see a PG13 movie when you're only ten. I said no because if the movie industry, which thinks it is ethical to bed down anything that moves, believes content warrants parental guidance for a child under thirteen, I would not be wise to wink at their judgment.

For a moment I thought I heard a voice say, "Okay, Mom, we realize you only have our best interests at heart.

We understand that learning a work ethic and delayed grati-
fication is an important part of becoming a mature adult."

Then I woke up.

Well, maybe someday they'll say that.

Sure, and maybe they'll turn their socks right-side-out
before throwing them in the laundry hamper, too.

Maybe someday they'll write me a long letter saying
they understand my life would have been a lot easier had I
chosen to be a Fun Mom, one who always said yes and sup-
plemented it with crisp green bills having denominations
ending in zero. They'll tell me how they appreciate the
energy, determination, and grit it took to be a No Mom, who
set a standard, clung to it, and made them earn their own
cash.

Maybe. And maybe they'll bring the basketballs into the
garage at night, too.

Until then, I will continue to say no. Because if it's a
choice between being my children's adored warm fuzzy, or
occasionally scowled and scorned because I teach some of
life's important lessons, I'll choose the latter.

When I have to choose between being my child's parent
or my child's friend, I am obliged to choose the role of parent. A friend is to commiserate with, sniff out the trends of
fashion with, and dream lofty dreams.

A mother is the one who may cause you to need someone to commiserate with, puts limits on the fashion trends,
and holds your feet to the earth. Popular or not, that's just
the way it is.

AFFLUENZA

Researchers have finally identified the latest virus threatening
American youth: affluenza. It will be entered in medical dic-
tionaries as follows:

THE HEART OF THINGS

af•flu•en•za: n : childhood disease caused by un-
precedented affluence and excess of materialism;
symptoms include irresponsibility, whining, and
incessant pleas of "gimme, gimme"; onset is typi-
cally in early childhood and, without early intervention, may last through adult years.

Freida Coddle stands on the porch of her lovely subur-
ban home as her family physician nails a "Quarantined for
Affluenza" sign to the front door.

Freida paces back and forth. An epidemic like this leaves
everyone running on black coffee and raw nerves. Three of the
four Coddle children are down with the virus. The baby
seems to have escaped. "Probably because he still sleeps most
of the day," the doctor explains. "It's good you called my
office when you did. How did you suspect affluenza?"

"Part luck, part intuition," says Freida. "I thought something was peculiar when Dudley left his brand-new mountain bike—the one we bought him for brushing his teeth two
days in a row—lying in the neighbor's yard for a week. But I
thought, 'Oh well, boys will be boys; he's only eight.'

"Then we found a hefty charge on the credit card bill
for a portable stereo CD player. Tiffany admitted she purchased it when she couldn't find fresh batteries for the old
one. The puzzling thing about that was we had just bought
her a sporty little convertible for her Sweet Sixteen birthday—she could have picked up batteries on one of the
dozen drives she made to the mall that week. But we don't
like to come down too hard on the kids.

"It was when Princess refused to leave her bedroom
because her favorite Ralph Booren T-shirt was in the laundry,
that I really got suspicious. I tried to coax her out with a
Fruit of the Loop one-pocket T, but she broke out in sweats
and chills at the poly-cotton blend and absolutely went to
pieces at the thought of something other than a designer

logo against her skin. She was sobbing, crying, and flailing about on her Dora Ashley canopy bed.

"That's when I called you."

"Hmmm. Good thing you did," the doctor said. "Affluenza is highly contagious. It's an airborne disease spread by casual contact through television airwaves, radio airwaves, shopping malls, and advertising circulars."

"How long before we can lift the quarantine?" Freida asked, her eyes now brimming with tears.

"Fourteen days," the doctor said. "They must have complete isolation—no exposure to any malls or media. After that they'll need a long-term maintenance program of curtailed television, a limited number of mail order catalogs, and closely monitored recreational shopping. And, Freida, I know this is going to be hard for you, but you need to try saying 'No,' once in awhile."

Freida grimaced at the thought. She blinked hard, sending two large tears cascading down her cheeks. "If we follow the prescribed treatment, do the kids have a good chance of recovery?" she asked with a sniff and a sob.

"We can't give guarantees," the doctor said. "We can give you sixty days same-as-cash on your outstanding bill, but we can't give guarantees. Once a child is infected with affluenza, it can be chronic. A diet pop commercial, even a stranger walking down the street in a trendy pair of blue jeans, can trigger a recurrence.

"Think about it, Freida, these affluneza germs have been incubating for years. You can't expect them to go away overnight."

CHARLOTTE'S FRIENDS

Charlotte's sin against her peers was that she was tall for her age and slightly overweight. She violated the range of acceptability as narrowly defined by *Seventeen* magazine.

Ever conscious of standards, a few kids on Bus 88 took it upon themselves, periodically, to remind Charlotte of her shortcomings. These self-appointed guardians of cool, kids with bangs over one eyebrow, hip clothes, and a knack for style, would some days tease Charlotte from the moment she lumbered aboard the bus. They ridiculed her shoes, mocked her pixie haircut, derided her parents—whom they'd never met—and her house, which they'd seen only from a distance.

Occasionally Charlotte would return fire, but most of the time she lost the war of insults, leaving the bus with her head hung low and her eyes brimming with tears.

There were other kids on that bus—regular old average kids who knew that the verbal attack was wrong. The afternoon ritual made them uneasy and uncomfortable. So they looked the other way.

Not a single adolescent mustered the courage to pipe up and say, "Hey, Charlotte, sit by me!" Not once, when Charlotte's face flushed and her chin quivered, did anyone give her a pat on the back and whisper, "Just ignore them." And not once did any of the regular kids dare tell the cool kids to stuff a sock in it. After all, age fourteen seemed too young to die.

The regular kids believed the cool kids controlled not only the bus and the cafeteria, but the universe as well. They had no idea that in a few short years the pecking order established in school would disappear overnight.

They could not envision the day they would no longer be riding Bus 88, or the day that Charlotte joined Weight Watchers, dropped twenty pounds, and matured into an attractive adult woman. Nor could they imagine the day when they would be in Charlotte's place, on the outside looking in, longing for a smidgen of encouragement from just one person.

People never find themselves permanently planted in the circle of acceptance. Be it in youth or adulthood, we all have occasions when we feel like Charlotte—a bit awkward, a tad self-conscious, or entirely out of place. Maybe we don't draw fire because we're too tall or too big. Maybe we're too short or too thin. Maybe we don't attract attention at all, but become invisible and ignored because we're too slow, too shy, too poor, or just too average.

Some of our most shameful moments occur when we let others languish in loneliness, when we overhear cruel taunts and we say nothing. Likewise, when we choose to speak up and say something, it is a moment when the power of one individual shines at its finest.

The power of one person patting the back of the kid chosen last for basketball can make that player feel like a member of the starting lineup. The power of one smile directed to that person fumbling to recover in the middle of an oral presentation can be just the spark she needs to finish the job. The power of one person seeking out the name that goes with the new face at the back of the crowd—and offering a handshake—can enhance the reputation of an entire town.

These aren't big things. They're little things that make a big difference. From time to time, we all need a gentle touch and an encouraging word—at Charlotte's age or any age.

COMMON SENSE, R.I.P.

Three yards of black fabric enshroud my computer terminal. I am mourning the passing of an old friend by the name of Common Sense.

His obituary reads as follows:

Common Sense, aka C.S., lived a long life, but died from heart failure at the brink of the millennium. No one really knows how old he was; his birth records were long ago entangled in miles and miles of bureaucratic red tape.

Known affectionately to close friends as Horse Sense and Sound Thinking, he selflessly devoted himself to a life of service in homes, schools, hospitals, and offices, helping folks get jobs done without a lot of fanfare, whooping, and hollering. Rules and regulations and petty, frivolous lawsuits held no power over C.S.

A most reliable sage, he was credited with cultivating the ability to know when to come in out of the rain, the discovery that the early bird gets the worm, and how to take the bitter with the sweet. C.S. also developed sound financial policies (don't spend more than you earn), reliable parenting strategies (the adult is in charge, not the kid), and prudent dietary plans (offset eggs and bacon with a little fiber and orange juice).

A veteran of the Industrial Revolution, the Great Depression, the Technological Revolution, and the Smoking Crusades, C.S. survived sundry cultural and educational trends, including disco, the men's movement, body piercing, whole language, and new math.

C.S.'s health began declining in the late 1960s when he became infected with the If-It-Feels-Good, Do-It virus. In the following decades his waning strength proved no match for the ravages of overbearing federal and state rules and regulations and an oppressive tax code. C.S. was sapped of strength and the will to live as the Ten Commandments became contraband, criminals received better treatment than victims, and judges stuck their noses in everything from Boy Scouts to professional baseball and golf.

His deterioration accelerated as schools implemented zero-tolerance policies. Reports of six-year-old boys charged with sexual harassment for kissing classmates, a teen suspended for taking a swig of Scope mouthwash after lunch, girls suspended for possessing Midol, and an honor student expelled for having a table knife in her school lunch were more than his heart could endure.

As the end neared, doctors say C.S. drifted in and out of logic but was kept informed of developments regarding regulations on low-flow toilets, mandatory air bags, and a government plan to ban inhalers from fourteen million asthmatics due to a trace of a pollutant that may be harmful to the environment. Finally, upon word that a North Carolina town council was attempting to restrict front porch furniture to lawn chairs and settees that are aesthetically attractive, C.S. breathed his last.

Services will be at Whispering Pines Cemetery. C.S. was preceded in death by his wife, Discretion; one daughter, Responsibility; and one son, Reason. He is survived by two stepbrothers, Half-Wit and Dim-Wit.

Memorial contributions may be sent to the Institute for Rational Thought.

Farewell, Common Sense. May you rest in peace. Hopefully, in a casket the state of North Carolina deems aesthetically attractive.

KIDS WITH EVERYTHING AND NOTHING

Susie and Billy have received nothing but the finest care and attention since birth. As babies, their designer diapers coordinated with their sleepers, and their room vaporizers were scented with cleansing mountain herbs.

As tots, they were kept on strict schedules for bedtime, meals, snacks, naps, and regular visits to the library, museum, and zoo. By early childhood, both kids were computer literate and played the piano at an intermediate level. Now in grade school, they can say hello, good-bye, please, and thank you in five different languages.

They are Super Kids in the making, a duo that will surely cure some dreaded disease, or at least invent a roll of toilet paper for public restrooms that won't break every two squares.

Every social, physical, and intellectual aspect of their development has been meticulously groomed and cultivated. They have received outstanding parenting, with one small exception.

Not once have they stepped foot inside a church or synagogue. Their intellectual development and physical conditioning zings off the scale, but their spiritual growth is flat-line. No one has explained God's love for them or prayed with them at bedtime. No one has told them about the creation of the heavens and the seas, the life of Abraham, or the journey of Moses.

Matthew, Mark, Luke, and John are just classmates at school. Jesus? They've seen that name somewhere—oh yes, on the name tag of the Hispanic guy who bags groceries at the store.

It's not like their folks didn't think about the spiritual dimension of life from time to time. It's just that there were always so many obstacles—number one being that church tends to be on Sundays. That's the only morning they have to relax from the rat race of running the kids to lessons, games, and extracurricular activities. Once they plow through the Sunday newspaper and watch some political round tables on television, it's time to leave for brunch. The Sunday timing has always been bad.

The folks pretty well settled on the idea that they would let their kids choose a faith for themselves when they were older, a little more mature. It would be something akin to shopping. When the kids felt the need for faith, they could browse around, try a few on, and select something that seemed comfortable.

Susie and Billy's parents never let them choose to ride their bikes on the interstate, but they're going to let them choose their own faith. They're going to let them choose whether they want to drift in a world of murky moral relativism or practice a living faith that has fortified individuals and families for centuries. Susie and Billy's family is not alone. According to a recent Gallup poll, only 38 percent of U.S. adults said they had gone to a church or synagogue within the last seven days.

One research psychologist has said that some religious influences are the mental equivalent of nuclear energy. Still, it is sometimes difficult to see the tangibles of spirituality. Sure, faith might affect the kids' choices on drinking and drugs, whom they date, and what they do on a date. Faith may even impact the quality of their marriages one day, inoculate them against depression, suicide, and speed their recovery from illnesses. Faith might be a powerful force in shaping personal character, yet some parents believe you can't force a thing like religion. It's private.

Not to worry. Susie and Billy are set. They are strong, healthy, and getting a decent education. They will surely excel on their SATs, sail through college, and land great jobs. After all, they're the kids who have been given everything.

Almost.

8

Shopping DAZE

'm glad there's no such thing as reincarnation. If there were, I am certain I would be sent back as a pooch—a happy, faithful, wet-nosed, four-legged friend. Which breed, I'm not sure, but a golden retriever comes quickly to mind. That, or a pointer or a setter, some breed that aptly personifies one of the primary expectations of me as a mom, the ability to fetch, retrieve, return, and deliver.

Retrieving may in fact be one of my best skills. I go to the mall, retrieve and return; the grocery, retrieve and return; the school, retrieve and return; the bank, retrieve and return. I doggedly pursue my prey through scorching heat, pelting rain, and blinding snow—though less and less often with my tongue a rosy pink and my tail wagging cheerfully.

JEAN JAMBOREE

The plan for Saturday was to lounge. Life was going according to schedule until shortly after lunch. Our son appears, announcing that he has had another growth spurt and needs new jeans.

"Prove it," I say.

117

"They cut into my stomach when I bend over."

"Touch your toes," I say.

He bends over, turns blue in the face, and passes out cold on the kitchen floor.

Great. Someone must take him to the mall. My husband has conveniently disappeared. I flag down the mailman and offer him cash to go shopping on my behalf. He claims it would violate his contract. Talk about a public servant with an attitude.

2:10: I drive the boy to the mall.

2:25: We enter a department store. He suggests we take the route that weaves through logo sportswear and athletic shoes. I insist we approach the jeans through housewares. And lingerie (like that really killed him).

2:30: We arrive at a regular Jean Jamboree. There are 98.7 trillion pairs of jeans in light blue, indigo blue, grunge blue, and manic-depressive blue.

2:31: I prop myself up against a support post next to a display of three mannequins and tell him I will wait here while he makes his selection.

Ten minutes pass. No sign of him. Two small children have checked the mannequins to see if they are wearing underwear.

2:45: A zealous sales clerk asks if she can help me. Twice.

2:50: Finally, my son ambles into view with his selection—one pair of jeans—and says he will try them on.

I join seven women loitering by the fitting rooms. One woman is fighting her son, who cannot be separated from his sweats. The kid bucks. The mom caves. They leave in a huff.

3:00: I am on a first-name basis with the remaining women waiting for sons to emerge from the fitting rooms. We have exchanged crock pot recipes for rolled pork loin. Still no sign of my kid.

The mother of a toddler has stuffed her child into knickers, suspenders, and a beanie hat, all of which resemble Little Lord Fauntleroy. It may not be tomorrow and it may not be next year, but from the look on the kid's face, he will one day seek revenge.

3:05: My son finally emerges from the fitting room. I ask him to lift his shirt so I may see the waist. He looks at me like I have asked him to run naked through the food court hawking pretzels and soft drinks.

3:10: It becomes obvious the one pair of jeans he has chosen do not fit. It also becomes obvious he is in no rush to find a pair that does fit.

3:13: Determined to return home in time to cosign our tax return by midnight April 15, I commence fetching assorted sizes and cuts of jeans and tossing them into the fitting room.

3:20: Student cut: too tight in the seat.

3:26: Relaxed cut: too baggy in the thighs.

3:32: Loose cut: too narrow at the ankles.

3:38: Generic brand: I am accused of trying to have my firstborn socially ostracized from his peers.

3:45: Bingo!

After only one hour and twenty minutes, we emerge from the department store with our package in tow. I only hope he doesn't have another growth spurt before we get to the car.

RESPECT THAT RECEIPT

You want a little respect?

Then save the receipt for every blasted thing you purchase.

I speak from experience: You're nobody without that one-by-three-inch piece of paper with the faded blue ink. Consider the following:

"I'd like to return this vacuum I purchased last night."

"Doesn't it run?" asks the clerk.

"Yes, it runs. The motor works fine. They just forgot to include the parts that pick up the dirt—the brushes, the roller, the belt."

"So what's the reason for return?"

Let me just add here that the clerk's name tag reads "Darla," but her voice says "Born to Punish."

"The reason for return is that this little vacuum has been gutted like a rainbow trout. The insides are gone."

"So you're saying it's not the wrong size, or the wrong color, you just don't want it?"

"Right, I get testy when a product labeled vacuum is unable to vacuum."

Then comes the killer. I've been waiting for it, dreading it, and feeling like a sneaky snake slithering through mud for the answer I must give.

"Do you have your receipt?" asks the Punisher.

"I did until this morning when the trash man came."

"WHAT? YOU DIDN'T SAVE YOUR RECEIPT?"

"No," I whimper in shame, "I didn't save my receipt."

The words "no receipt" cause blood to concentrate in the Punisher's face. Obviously, the Punisher would like me better if I admitted to slashing tires on wheelchairs or hating kittens, bunnies, and small babies wearing white eyelet bonnets. But no, I have committed the unpardonable consumer sin: I have not saved my receipt.

Ironically, I have been selectively saving receipts for years. It just turns out I've selected the wrong ones to save.

Every receipt for car maintenance and repair is in an envelope in the car's glove box. Silly shopper! Like a mechanic is going to rip apart the engine a second time just because there's still a knock under the hood and I have the receipt. Equally stupid is the file folder containing receipts for medical expenses. Like we're going to get a cash refund for Amoxicillin that didn't take out an ear infection in ten days.

A repairman recently asked if I had the receipt for a garage door spring he replaced five years ago. I patted down my pockets, but no receipt. Caught again.

It is critical to save receipts for products that you think are going to last and you would never dream of returning, like a pair of $54 boy's shoes (which by the way were worn only four weeks before the tops separated from the sides).

Save receipts on anything guaranteed to be durable or waterproof. You can count on it falling apart and leaking. Save the receipt on everything that promises to be "tuff." What kind of quality control can you expect from a company that can't spell?

It is mandatory to save receipts on anything a kid could touch, wear, or fire through the air like a football.

To be safe, save the receipt for everything you buy. It'll take an extra day each week, fifty-two days a year, and seven years out of your life just to gather receipts and organize them, but hey, you were just sitting around with nothing to do, waiting for something to break anyway.

Think of the satisfaction when your purchase falls apart at the seams. You may have bought a lemon, but at least you can put your hands on the lousy receipt.

RED PLAID RITUAL

I'm a sucker for red plaid. Red and green laced with thin black stripes kindles childhood memories of fall shopping trips in my home state of Nebraska.

Every September, my Great-Aunt Ruth and I would board a bus headed for the throbbing heart of downtown Lincoln. Naturally, one would dress appropriately for such a special occasion. Aunt Ruth would change from her "everyday" shirtwaist print dress into her "good" shirtwaist print dress. She would then tuck her white gloves, freshly ironed hankie, and box of Sucrets into her sturdy brown pocketbook and snap it shut with the shiny gold clasp.

We would wait on the southwest corner of St. Paul Avenue and 43rd Street for the downtown bus, which was always on schedule. The bus would rumble to a halt and the door would screech open, then huff shut as soon as we boarded. It carried us on our journey, belching exhaust and jerking to a stop every three blocks, picking up new passengers and allowing others to depart.

Once at our destination, we strode directly to Miller and Paine's department store, where the click of women's high heels echoed on hardwood floors and the scent of gardenias floated from the cosmetics counter. Uniformed elevator attendants in maroon jackets with shiny brass buttons, perched on upholstered stools, diligently saw to it that we reached our desired floor.

After purchasing a new school dress—which was always red plaid, no discussion, no questions asked—we would then board the bus for home. Shopping was an Event.

The ritual of purchasing that red plaid dress added rhythm to life. That shopping trip produced more than a dress with a full skirt and a white Peter Pan collar; it heralded the arrival of fall. It was a signal crimson leaves would be falling soon, followed by yellow and rust chrysanthemums in bloom and the appearance of big pumpkins carved with crooked teeth and triangular eyes.

Most events of that magnitude have all but disappeared from today's hectic calendars. Shopping is no longer an event, but a continuous 'round-the-clock hobby, an alleged addiction for some.

Grocery stores were branded radical when they first opened their doors on Sunday afternoons. Now, twenty-four-hour-a-day operations are routine. Even drugstores, discount stores, and copying centers have followed suit. Our local hardware store has a contractors' office open "mornings, afternoons, and evenings" seven days a week. As Christmas approaches (ever considerate of our holiday shopping needs), the giant toy supermarkets will be staying open until midnight.

Purchases are rarely preceded by great anticipation or planning, let alone scrimping and saving. All that's truly needed today is a touch-tone phone and a plastic card with a distant expiration date.

While shopping has mushroomed into a nonstop activity, other events have come to a virtual standstill. Letter-writing and leisurely chatting over tea have been rendered nearly obsolete by the speed and efficiency of computerized greeting cards, e-mail, beepers, car phones, and fax machines.

Eating and drinking traditions are following a similar route to the endangered species list. The family dinner hour has succumbed to the speed of single-serving microwave meals that can be easily devoured while standing upright. We not only eat in a hurry, we drink in a hurry as well.

Not so long ago, someone sipping coffee from a foam cup was usually a victim of distress—a family member waiting in a hospital emergency room or a harried doctor in a rush. Today, we're all on the run nursing a variety of beverages from oversized plastic cups, travel mugs, or glass bottles with screw tops. Either dehydration is epidemic or life itself has become one prolonged emergency.

Shopping, eating, and conversing are no longer Events, but continuums with no end or beginning. In the name of convenience, we can do it all with no notice, planning, or forethought, twenty-four hours a day, seven days a week. Day after day after day.

Perhaps we haven't lost the rhythm of life. The rhythm has simply changed.

SURFING FOR BARGAINS

I am the type of computer user you would call on for technical expertise only if you had been drinking heavily. I know you don't bait the mouse with D-Con and that "booting up" the computer does not involve Tony Lama, but I am a far cry from a computer geek who memorizes software licensing agreements for cyber grins ;-)

Credentials, or lack of them, aside, a friend and her sister recently asked if I would do them a computer favor. My friend and her sister, both of whom are unfamiliar with the Internet, are highly educated, intelligent women (and to the best of my knowledge do not drink). One owns her own business and the other is a successful attorney, although I try not to hold that against her. They are precisely the type of sophisticated women who would want to surf the Net for the latest information on stocks and bonds, technology, medical research, and federal legislation.

Naturally, I assumed they needed something fairly urgent and specific. Indeed they did. They wanted to find out how to sell a Beanie Babie named Spooky on the Internet.

Spooky says a lot about the Internet. Of course, it says even more about Internet users when you learn there are 21,500 Web sites featuring Beanie Babies. As you may have deduced, many Internet users have an inordinate amount of time on their hands. All in all, it is probably best that those type folks are glued to computer screens rather than wandering loose on our city streets.

To the people like my friends who are intimidated by the Internet, I would like to remove a bit of the mystique. Going on-line does not involve electrical shocks. Surfing requires no swimwear, and downloading does not mean bending from the knees when dropping your end of a heavy appliance.

In truth, the Internet is primarily a female medium—it is nothing more than pure and simple shopping. Picture the

Internet as a global mall, flea market, and sidewalk sale combined, and you've got the concept. Search software is nothing more than an on-screen directory, like the map in a box at the mall with a red arrow indicating "You are here."

Stay with me, ladies, and I can have you Net-friendly in another three graphs.

What's the first thing you do when you go shopping? Right: You cruise the lot and blow time looking for a parking spot. Same for the Net. You listen to a busy signal through a modem and read a box that says you have an unreliable terminal connection before your computer finally finds an open spot.

After parking, your next move is to enter the store and approach a clerk for help. And the clerk does what? Exactly. Picks up her purse and goes on break. Same for the Net. You type in the item or topic you want to locate and prepare for a brief wait.

The clerk can't help you find the item you want, but she can direct you to the southeast corner of Sportswear. Same for the Net. It may not find the exact thing you asked for, but it will give you several thousand choices to sort through. You click the mouse and open document after document, only to realize this feels remarkably similar to shopping clearance sales. Each document opens slower than the one before, allowing you to vacuum the house, do forty stomach crunches, and address Christmas cards between documents. Like shopping, the browsing grows tedious and the merchandise sometimes appears shopworn and disheveled, but once you find the right size and color, you know it was worth the hunt.

Of course, a simple shopping analogy is in no way intended to minimize the phenomenal powers of the Internet that link the sharpest minds around the world, enabling them to exchange highly technical information with dazzling speed. How else could I learn that on Saturday Spooky was selling for $40 and today you can find a buyer willing to pay at least $45?

DRESSING ROOM REVENGE

I just wanted to confirm that it was indeed my daughter you heard laughing with wild abandon in the department store dressing room last week. Since I no longer have any personal pride left, I feel duty-bound to go public with the entire episode to prevent other women from similar humiliation.

One of my daughters accompanied me to shop for a dress. As I bent over to step into dress number one, I will admit my belly button was momentarily eclipsed by a roll of skin. Or as she calls it, "FAT."

"Mom, your belly button just disappeared. Aren't you worried?"

I ignored her but thought to myself, if I was worried about padding around my waist, your brother would have been an only child. Besides, this was a kid who barely weighs fifty-five pounds and the only fat she's ever carried is still in her little cherub cheeks.

I hurriedly tried on a second dress, knowing that all the fitting rooms were occupied and several people were waiting. Once again, as I bent over, my belly button was obscured. "Mom, it just disappeared again, that is sooooooo gross!" Now mind you, this is not a tire around my waist that would fit a John Deere tractor, but apparently it was enough to make her snicker.

The snicker grew into a giggle, which I met head-on with a cold glare. The glare was intimidating; she responded with a belly laugh. I countered with pursed lips making a threatening "ssshhhhhhh" sound. That was it—her belly laugh burst into a loud, high-pitched howl as she totally lost control, slid down the dressing room wall, shaking the full-length mirrors, and collapsed on the floor convulsing with uncontrollable laughter.

The efficient sales clerk rapped on the door, "Everything all right, dear? Would you like a different size, a different color perhaps?"

No, just a different shopping partner—preferably someone over ninety with no muscle tone and a weakness for cheesecake.

Actually, we were just perfecting a family tradition. My mom and I did some of our best bantering in dressing rooms.

"It's ugly."

"It's cute."

"Why are you trying to make me look like a football player?"

"Puff sleeves and lace trim are very feminine."

"You make me wear this to school and ten-to-one they'll have me in the varsity lineup Friday night."

My mother's warning of, "Someday...someday...just you wait and see," was now coming to pass. My young shopping companion freely critiques my lingerie. She asks if I can do anything about my legs and whether I'll be getting any taller. Occasionally she even spots something she thinks would look nice—on a blonde.

It's poetic justice for the snide observations I made about middle-aged women when I was her age. I was fascinated (okay, maybe it was more like repulsed) by the bulging veins on their hands. Now my own hands are beginning to look like a relief map of the Mississippi River and her tributaries. Don't think my kids haven't noticed and delivered commentary.

I used to marvel at how soft and squishy Aunt Ceila's upper arms were when she'd engulf me in a hug. And even though I faithfully lift my twenty-ounce cans of crushed pineapple twice a week, I suspect in another few years my kids will probably force me to register my own hanging flab as a lethal weapon.

I still recommend mothers take their daughters shopping—but only after issuing them a cautionary warning: Feel free to enter the dressing room with me, but before you deliver an unsolicited critique, remember this—I may be heavily armed.

UNDERWEAR HAPPINESS

You never realize how much the success of your day hinges on underwear until you study the advertising circulars.

Right now, I am looking at a picture of a man who is the thirty-ninth Tom Cruise look-alike I have seen in an advertisement this week. He is wearing an all-cotton V-neck T-shirt, an all-cotton brief, a button-down shirt hanging open, and a tie draped around his neck. He is holding his morning cup of hot coffee and wearing a look of total confidence. This go-get-'em businessman who has the world by the tail is grinning from ear to ear—and is totally oblivious to the fact that he is not wearing any pants.

My husband and I could never get away with eating breakfast half-clothed. For one thing, we both feel much safer pouring hot coffee or frying bacon when we are fully dressed. Secondly, such a sight would startle the kids.

Our children aren't as relaxed as the kids in these ads. Take the boy and girl, about eleven years of age, pictured romping about in their skivvies, swinging a pillow at one another. Apparently, they don't have a clue that prancing around like that could one day make them regulars at a therapist's office. They look so giddy, it makes you wonder if a different brand of undershirt really can bring a family closer together.

Football great Joe Montana and his wife, Jennifer, always looked so happy in their advertisements for T-shirts and briefs. But was it the underwear or the modeling fees that made them so effervescent?

I've also wondered how one brand of undergarments can bring some models such happiness, while another line of the identical article of clothing brings other models such torment. I have seen lingerie—expensive garments tailored for a custom fit from comfortable fabrics—that make grown women snarl. Some of these models have one eyebrow arched, others have flared nostrils. All of them have a curled lip that sneers, "Who let the vermin with the camera in the room?"

I could understand the look had they been partially dressed, minding their own business in the privacy of their kitchen, when photographers showed up unexpectedly. Most women, naturally, would be very irritated and dive for cover behind the refrigerator door or fan out the newspaper for extra coverage. Yet these photo sessions were obviously planned and the women still look miffed.

Even fully clothed models look agitated. The teens in Calvin Klein ads looked positively sullen. I've never known a new pair of jeans to render kids so forlorn and miserable. It must be a trend.

I attended a style show where all the models stormed down the runway in brand-new clothes looking as though they could lunge off the stage and body slam the audience. They stomped back and forth with a gait remarkably similar to the high-step marching of Hitler's Brown Shirts.

The woman next to me said her nine-year-old daughter recently stomped downstairs to breakfast with that same demeanor. "I told her to get right back upstairs and not to come back until she wiped that nasty look off her face."

That's good advice for models, too. If they detest their jobs so much that they can't look semi-pleasant, they ought to change careers—or at least try a happier brand of underwear.

ACCIDENT ON AISLE TWO

The only contribution my right hand can make in this typing effort is an occasional muscle spasm that sends my index finger lurching to the number row of the key7board with no 3warning.

The reason is, I had a little accident. You know how 9people scrimp and save and take a little jaunt to ski the slopes at Vail—only to come back with a souvenir in the form of a cast and sling? Well that's not what happened to me. 88888888 That kind of accident would be glamorous.

My accident happened much closer to home. On level 339ground. At the grocery store. You don't ordinarily think of the grocery store as a dangerous place, but it is. Trust me. I've got the immobilized hand458 and tingling fingers to prove it.

My cart and I were hit broadside by a muscular, towering clerk on a dead run for the customer service counter. The force of the blow was so severe it jerked the cart from my hands, sprained my wrist, and nearly straightened all four wheels on the cart.

I admit to part of the blame. I was going the wrong way through an empty one-way express lane in order to save ten steps. I was in a hurry.

There's something about the grocery store on a weekend that turns ordinary, mild-mannered people prone to dally into crazed, frenzied maniacs. Maybe it's the two-for-one specials, the double coupons, or the free pizza samples. Maybe there's just an electrifying force generated by a crowded store with too few checkers, long snaking lines, and the incessant beep of the scanner that subliminally screams, "Run, baby, run—that rump roast for $1.98 a pound ain't gonna last forever!"

Monday through Friday, the grocery seems spacious, roomy enough to comfortably double-park to ponder the iceberg, Bibb, and Boston lettuce. Monday through Friday, the grocery is so leisurely and friendly that a shopper feels free to block the dairy aisle while checking the expiration date on the cottage cheese.

But on Saturdays, the grocery feels as packed as one of those rallies the communists used to have in Red Square to salute Lenin. On Saturdays, it's as though the instant the automatic door swings open, an invisible force warns shoppers to either beat the crowd or be beaten. I've got a hunch the clerks feel it, too.

Accidentally give a clerk an expired coupon on a Wednesday and she's forgiving. Pass one on a Saturday and she acts like you were trying to steal money from a sock full of coins she'd been saving for her invalid mother.

This being a weekend, feeling intense pressure to rush my bargains to the car, I veered to the checkout lane with the shortest line—manned by the fellow whom minutes earlier I had pinned with my cart. Holding my injured right arm Napoleon-style and throwing groceries on the belt with my left, I asked him if he recognized me.

"Sure, you're the woman who tried to break both my legs with your cart," he said.

"I sure feel sorry about that," I said. "I bet that hurt."

"It sure did," he said, smacking the "total" button on the cash register. "But don't feel too sorry for me. I just over-charged you on all your groceries."

That 8would nev7er happen on a Monday98886567.

9

Are We Having FUN Yet?

There are two kinds of vacations: Brochure Vacations and Real Vacations. On Brochure Vacations everything is pre-planned and falls neatly into place. You reserve the beautiful room with a view six months in advance, and guarantee it with your credit card. The travel agency sends you a suggested packing list and full-color pictures of the gift shoppe. The hotel prearranges recreation activities for the kiddos and identifies six restaurants guaranteed to have clean silverware and even cleaner restrooms.

On a Real Vacation you wing it a lot. You veer off the beaten path and drive winding, hilly backroads. The engine develops a terrible knock and you coast into a desolate gas station, only to find it manned by two fellas straight out of *Deliverance*. On a Real Vacation you drive miles and miles after dark, hoping and praying for a vacancy sign before daybreak. On a Real Vacation you make at least one stop at a Wal-Mart because someone forgot underwear, someone else lost their swimsuit, and Dad ran out of film.

Our best vacations always involved at least two minor disasters, one really filthy restaurant, and a truly good row over who should read the atlas and who should just be quiet and drive.

We considered a Brochure Vacation once, but we chickened out. We were afraid the boredom would kill us.

JOY RIDE

You've probably read a lot of fascinating information on how to travel with children. Naturally, you've wondered two things: exactly how these books crawled from the fantasy section of the bookstore to the travel section, and how to breed children who are entertained by alphabetizing license plates of out-of-state motorists.

Unfortunately, you won't find answers to those questions, because the authors of these books and articles are unreachable. They're globe-trotting by private jets this summer. For amusement, they swoop low over interstates to view a family traveling cross-country by car. Its occupants are knee-deep in cookie crumbs, with a delirious parent frantically rubbing ice cubes over bubble gum stretched the entire width of a backseat. After a hearty laugh, the travel expert ascends back to 33,000 feet, cruises at 700 mph, enjoys surround-sound stereo, and relaxes in a Jacuzzi.

I believe the key to successful automobile travel with children (successful being defined as reaching your destination with the same number of passengers you left with) is to remember this: Kids respect a stranger in uniform.

That's why I've found it helpful to don an old blond wig and a double-breasted navy blue blazer with United Airlines junior pilot wings on the lapel moments after my passengers board the minivan. Once the kids are buckled into place, I lower my voice two octaves and huskily announce, "Hi, I'm Stacey and I'll be your hostess today.

"Please be informed that maternal regulations forbid the transport of concealed rodents, reptiles, rocks, and any and all chocolate that melts in your hand, not in your mouth. All carry-on luggage, including Barbie accessories and Legos, must be stored under your seat until takeoff.

"Our estimated time of arrival will fluctuate wildly depending on the stability of the interpersonal relationships within the vehicle. We hope you enjoy your trip."

Then, with a frozen smile and my index and middle fingers forming graceful V's, I make dramatic sweeping gestures indicating the nearest windows in the event of unforeseen car sickness resulting in projectile vomiting.

It's not a bad routine. It often mesmerizes the kids into making polite predeparture chatter discussing the odds on my rattling back with a beverage cart and smoked almonds. But once they realize that the turbulence is from chuckholes and that there will be no in-flight movie, things can turn ugly pretty fast.

The feats a woman under stress can perform at a thirty-second stoplight are truly amazing. My personal best was triggered by a bloodcurdling scream and a choking sound. I threw the gearshift into park, spiraled into the middle seat, and plucked from the baby's tongue a stray piece of Easter egg grass that was triggering her gag reflex. Sailing on into the backseat, I loosened my son's stranglehold on a shock of his sister's blond hair and quickly applied pressure to her superficial scalp wound while threatening him with the possibility of completing the trip strapped to the luggage rack.

All that accomplished within a cool 27.9 seconds, I vaulted back into the driver's seat. The light turned green. I pushed the pedal to the metal and glanced in my rearview mirror. The driver behind me was cheering wildly and waving a card bearing the score 9.7.

Not all sibling assault and battery can be brought under control that swiftly. Sometimes conditions warrant a cool-headed navigator spending miles negotiating with an on-board terrorist holding Barbie's bicycle shorts hostage in exchange for a window seat.

Travel experts abhor parents who bargain with such culprits. They recommend directing an air-conditioning vent toward the crazed passenger as a soothing tactic. I score that a 4. This expert says cut a deal and cut it quickly. What's a cold soft drink and bag of mini-pretzels in the name of interstate peace?

FIGHT FOR THE FRONT SEAT

If God had intended families to take lengthy automobile trips with children, He would have equipped parents with necks that rotate 360 degrees and elastic arms.

Heads capable of total revolutions would make it much easier to accommodate passengers who shriek, "LOOK, MOM! QUICK! LOOK!" A swiveling head would enable the driver to verify the species of three-day-old road kill without barreling over the yellow line and careening down an embankment at 65 mph.

Elastic arms able to stretch twenty-three times beyond normal human capabilities would make it easier to pinch the chubby thighs of sassy passengers and open the cooler wedged behind the driver's seat without dislocating a shoulder.

Still, not even swiveling heads and elastic arms come close to solving the major flash point of every trip—the mystery of the backseat. The backseat has a puzzling ability to ignite antagonism, bickering, and all-out war.

My husband and I, who routinely sit in the front seat, have never once jabbed one another in the ribs for looking out each other's window. But in the backseat, this occurs with predictability. My husband and I have never made long squiggly lines on each other's legs with a purple marker because we perceived a silent sneer. This also has been known to happen with annoying frequency in the backseat.

In the interest of behavioral science, I'm considering relocating to the backseat on the next family trip—but only reluctantly. The danger is that once you sit in the backseat, kids make the erroneous assumption that the front passenger seat is up for grabs.

Make no mistake—it is not. The front passenger seat always has been, and always will be, the queen's throne. It may not look like red velvet to you, but it is a position of privilege. Repeatedly, I tell children who challenge me for the front passenger seat that I have earned that privilege three times over.

"After any one of you barrel through swinging doors leading to a hospital delivery room three times and encounter the thrill of stainless steel stirrups, then, and only then, will you become eligible for the queen's throne. At that time, window control, air vent positions, glove box maintenance, and the radio dial can be all yours—but until then, they are mine. So get in and get in the back."

Naturally, desiring to sample the royal lifestyle, whenever I drive the kids somewhere, the seating arrangement becomes a GM passenger version of King of the Mountain. Equipped with hearing keener than dogs, children have been known to discern the jingle of car keys and the low rumble of a garage door rolling up from six blocks away. The kid with the sharpest hearing and fastest reflexes is the winner who proudly occupies the front passenger seat. Losers move to the back and sulk.

So how is it, whenever I drive somewhere with just one child, that child will predictably open the car door and quietly buckle into the backseat? Only after talking, coaxing, and occasionally bribing, will the child move to the front.

When you want kids to sit in the back, they clamor to ride up front. When you want them in the front, they climb in the back.

Since the puzzle of the backseat continues to be a vexing mystery, perhaps the dilemma could best be solved if the steering wheel and dashboard were simply relocated to the back. Of course, once you did that, the kids would naturally all want to sit in the front. Oh, fine. Just don't get any cookie crumbs on that red velvet or mess with the scepter.

POSTCARDS FROM THE EDGE—OF NEBRASKA

Dear Buffy,
Flying coach to Hilton Head must have been miserable for you. At least you'll have four weeks to recover in your ocean-view condo with the Jacuzzi. It took us two days and 740 miles, but we made it to the family reunion here in Hickman, Nebraska (that's south of Denton and west of Palmyra). Met in a field—real hot. Were thankful for the seedling pine tree and strip of shade cast by the port-a-potty. Everybody looked great. No big changes. The truck of choice is still Ford, the hat of choice John Deere, and the favorite hobby is still eating. Aunt Judy's boy rode a bull at a rodeo last night, where the girls learned to crack sunflower seeds and spit shells cowboy-style. We head out tomorrow. "Colorado or Bust!"

Dear Vicki,
Crossed Nebraska with only thirty-seven bathroom stops. Two of the kids got a little woozy—staring at endless fields of corn whizzing by at 65 mph does

137

that. Saw hay bales shaped like giant loaves of
bread, and on several occasions the Platte River
crossed from the north to the south side of the
interstate. Grandma and Grandpa are traveling
along with us in their van with our two nephews.
We talked back and forth part of the way by walkie-
talkies till the kids ran the batteries down telling
stupid jokes, making choking noises, and scanning
the channels for truckers. Can't wait to see photos
of your Alaskan cruise when we get back. I didn't
know they offered vacation packages for adults
only.

Dear Katy,
Received your picture postcards of Liberty Bell,
Kitchen Utensils of George Washington's Third
Cousin, and Continental Congress Fountain Pen
Collection before we left. You're so good at making
history come alive for the children. We tricked our
kids into going to the Denver Mint. Waited in line
forty minutes. Looked like we were next, but then a
tour bus pulled up. Herds of senior citizens got off
and swarmed inside ahead of us. We were pulling
Danny off the spiked fence, ready to call it quits,
when we heard sirens. A fire truck and two squad
cars roared up to the building across the street.
Firefighters jumped out with oxygen tanks and
huge axes. It was a false alarm, but the kids had a
really good time after all.

Dear Susan,
After driving for two days, we finally spotted majestic snowcapped peaks yesterday about 2 P.M. Kids
were sound asleep. Did a little hiking. We hear the
headaches subside and breathing gets easier at high

altitudes the more time you spend outside. Isn't this elk postcard majestic? Bought a second card for myself, as we haven't seen a single one. We've stepped on a lot of their calling cards though— natives call them Elk Duds. Saw a hoary marmot. It's somewhere between a groundhog and a squirrel on steroids. More hiking tomorrow (providing we get the burrs out of the shoes and socks tonight and the headaches subside). Should be great fun. Pray those forest fires stay to the south and west. Tell Mickey and Minnie hello when you get to Disney World.

Dear Cyndi,
I'm eager to see the napkin collection from your Around the World in Forty Restaurants vacation when we return. We're dining *al fresco*. We hit the road with our trusty Coleman PolyLite 48 cooler and a box filled with staples like pretzels, peanut butter, and powdered donuts. We're now in the parking lot of Eisenhower's birthplace in Abilene, Kansas, eating our third meal today of Special K (we finished the bagels, yogurt, and vegetable sticks leaving the Rockies). *Bon appétit!*

Dear Jen,
We'll be home soon. Our time in Colorado was great. Warm days, cool nights, no humidity—perfect! I also enjoyed no phone, no dishes, and no washing machine. The kids' highlight was the motel pool. Suppose it would have been cheaper to stay home, buy a pool pass, pull the plug on the phone, ban laundry, and refuse to cook. But then we would have missed the joy of 2,200 miles together in the car. You can't buy memories like that.

VACATION VOTED MOST BORING

When my husband and I mentioned the possibility of a trip to an educational spot like Colonial Williamsburg, the response from the kids was unanimous:

"I have friends who went to Williamsburg," said the thirteen-year-old. "They almost didn't make it back."

"Problem?" I asked.

"Big one. They nearly died of boredom."

Like all kind and caring parents, we would never bombard our children with lethal doses of boredom. We would, however, settle for a few days of moderate discomfort. Say, drag them around Washington, D.C., and expose their impressionable brains to the history of our nation's capital.

Of course, we know a decision like this will cost us popularity points, but that doesn't matter. What matters is that as parents we possess keen powers of persuasion, powers that enable us to say things like, "Get in the car and get ready to have a good time whether you want to or not."

It was no surprise that our powers of persuasion were tested from time to time. The first challenge came when we commenced a lively self-guided walking tour of Memorials and Monuments Made of Large Slabs of Stone.

Kid: "You mean we have to get out of the car? We thought just you and Dad were going."

Parent (persuasively): "Think again."

Kid: "Why can't you just leave us the keys to the car and let us listen to the radio?"

Parent (blending persuasion and intimidation): "We didn't drive six hundred miles so you could sit in the car and listen to the radio."

Kid: "What if we listened to NPR?"

Parent (using full-force persuasion): "GET OUT OF THE CAR, NOW!"

140

After three days of nonstop walking and touring, we all acquired blisters, shin splints, and acute leg cramps. The kids claim that was the fun part. Eventually, they did warm to the idea of exploring the nation's capital, as evidenced by the moment one of them yelled, "WOWWW!"

"What is it?" I asked, looking up from the tour map. "The Washington Monument, the Reflecting Pool?"

"Look! In the alley! A candy apple red Commando Jeep with whitewall tires and a convertible top."

So it went. We dragged them through Ford's Theater, where President Lincoln was assassinated, and all they remember is that it was a dark and dingy auditorium only a hop, skip, and jump from the Hard Rock Cafe.

We herded them through the Smithsonian, past the Enola Gay, and pressed their noses to the glass to view the collection of First Ladies' ball gowns. What did they see? The shirtless tattooed guy at the entrance to the museum with a boa constrictor wrapped around his neck.

We propped them up for pictures in front of the White House, the Roosevelt Memorial, and the Capitol building. What did they want a picture of? An albino squirrel in Pershing Park.

We continued walking long after the sun had set, showing them the city reflected at dusk in the Potomac and the Supreme Court awash in floodlights. The night scene that caught their attention most? Two tawdry hookers working the street beneath our hotel window.

Parent (using maximum persuasion): "HEY! You kids get away from that window. I SAID GET AWAY FROM THE WINDOW, NOW!"

Kids (fighting to crawl beneath the draperies and reclaim view of the street): "But you said we were here to take in the sights. You told us to keep our eyes open. You told us to enjoy the sights of our national heritage!"

Parent: "This is Washington, kids. You can't believe everything you hear."

WHAT'S SO GREAT ABOUT
THE GREAT OUTDOORS?

Nothing draws a family together like hiking in the Great Outdoors. Mosquitoes the size of blue herons, slithering water snakes, and blood-sucking ticks have a way of fostering a special kind of closeness.

Hiking is a family activity now regarded as an enjoyable hobby only because we no longer are forced to hike everywhere out of necessity. Grunt work has a way of becoming fun once it is optional.

Even so, hiking is an outdoor pastime that still requires a lot of slick marketing and packaging to disguise the fact that it is actually hard work. For example, if you asked a room full of intelligent people how many of them would like to venture into the wilderness during peak heat and sweat like pigs, burn their flesh to a crisp, walk until their arches fell flat, and scrape the backs of their thighs raw sliding down slippery ravines, maybe one or two hands would give a faltering half-wave in the air.

On the other hand, if you asked the same people who would like to purchase rugged, but fashionable, outdoor wear from an L.L. Bean catalog, breathe fresh pine-scented air, improve their tans, and wrap themselves in the wonders of nature while hiking, the entire room would pulsate as arms waved wildly in the air. Even when you told these people they would spend the entire day walking in a perfect circle, they would still agree to go.

Personally, I think hiking would gain even more popularity if parks did away with those nature centers. The graphic displays on brown recluse spiders, ticks carrying Lyme disease, and coyotes don't exactly lure throngs of city folks into the woods.

The park personnel always put a positive spin on all the critters by saying, "Remember, they're just as scared of you as you are of them." Right. And it is also possible to run into Bambi, Thumper, and the Seven Dwarfs along the trail.

I can take about two days of getting back to nature before I must get back to civilization. After forty-eight hours of dirt under my fingernails, I will gladly exchange a sagging tent and lukewarm cooler for a blast of air conditioning and a flush toilet. I am spellbound by people who willingly give up refrigerators, stoves, and queen-size beds to camp for an entire week. For an "enjoyable outing," camping requires an enormous amount of planning, packing, austerity, and self-denial.

What's even more amazing is that some people cheerfully pay other people big bucks to deprive them of the comforts of home. Take the brochure with the beautiful picture of a line of horseback riders silhouetted against a ruby red sunset: "Join us on an old-fashioned trail drive. Enjoy a primitive ten days of horseback riding, herding cattle, beans by the fire, and a bedroll under the stars, $775 per person."

Have you ever seen a tour group on horseback returning to their home base? They are caked with dust and wobble like wet noodles in their saddles. Every one of them looks like they are recovering from a branding iron to their backside. Their faces are forlorn, pathetic, and pitiful.

I think someone ought to pay me for following cow pies, torturing my gastrointestinal system, and subjecting myself to muscle spasms by sleeping on gravel.

My idea of experiencing nature at its best is a short hike on a well-worn trail—that leads directly to a Holiday Inn with fresh towels and an indoor pool.

10

Let's TALK

A friend says it isn't that her husband doesn't *want* to talk in the evenings, it's just that by the time he gets home from work, he has run out of words.

I've known couples like that. What am I saying? We are a couple like that. One night at dinner, my worn-out husband, who had barely spoken a word the entire meal, looked at me and snapped, "What are we going to do about this problem?"

"What problem?" I asked. "You never mentioned a problem."

"She's not eating her dinner," he said, gesturing toward our resident food picker. "And I *did* say something."

"Well, I sure didn't hear you," I said.

"I told you with my eyes," he said.

"Huh?" I responded.

"Three times I looked at you and three times I looked at her plate," he said. "You looked right at me like you knew what I was talking about."

"Let me get this straight," I said, shaking my head. "I looked at you like I knew what you were talking about with your eyes?"

"Exactly!" he barked.

There are two ways to look at this scenario. Either our communication skills are so lousy that we will soon be interviewed for "Can This Marriage Be Saved?" article, or we communicate so well that we're beyond the point of even needing words. Now *that's* close.

SPEECHLESS

My greatest fear before getting married was that my husband and I would run out of things to talk about. We racked up hefty phone bills during our early courtship, but that was because we lived in different states, worked at different newspapers, had different sets of friends, and ate different frozen food entrées.

What could two people possibly have to talk about when they lived not only in the same city, but in the same house, saw the same friends, and ate the same meals?

"What's new?" would no longer be an exciting question necessitating a rambling forty-five-minute answer. In my personal worst-case scenario, our marriage would last six months before it languished in desperate need of professional counseling.

The marriage counselor would begin by asking, "What's new?"

"Nothing," I'd say.

"Not much," my beloved would agree.

"Is there something you'd like to talk about today?" the therapist would continue probing.

"Not really," my husband would say.

"Nope," I'd chime in.

And so it would go, until the session ended with a bang—which would come from the counselor's head crashing on his desktop due to the lethal boredom generated by such a dearth of lively conversation.

Little did I know, as a single person, that conversation opportunities increase in direct proportion to the number of years a couple has been married. Most couples pass through a natural conversational evolution of people, places, and things.

Newlyweds talk about people: each other, themselves, her mother, his mother, his friends, her friends, each other, and themselves. Couples married for a few years, having accumulated a little pocket change, talk about the places they go, the movies they see, and the restaurants where they dine.

Once a couple has assumed the responsibilities of a house and children, their conversations are monopolized by things: things that are broken, in the process of breaking, or beyond repair. These couples have fascinating conversations about leaky gutters, termites, insurance policies, a magazine fund-raiser, catalytic converters, storm windows, and bathroom faucets.

The true masters of conversation are couples like my in-laws, who have been married nearly fifty years. Once, during a commercial break in a televised Chicago Cubs' game, they discussed a relief pitcher who stinks, the death of Orville Redenbacher, the price of seed corn, and the value of clipping coupons. It was reminiscent of a tennis match—he lobbed, she returned, he lobbed, she returned. They hit four subject matters in what appeared to be a logical fashion, all before the completion of station identification. You don't master conversational skills like that overnight.

My husband and I, still in the home-and-child-responsibilities cycle, have found there is no dearth of things to talk about—just a dearth of time in which to talk about them. Conversations must be squeezed in through shower doors, over the blare of radios, wailing children, and tennis balls banging against the garage door. We talk in snippets squeezed between trips to the library and phone interruptions. We scrawl notes on napkins for one another and discuss current events by cutting up the newspaper, leaving articles of interest by the coffeemaker and cartoons tacked to the fridge. It's gotten so bad at times that we have had to make dates in order to have an uninterrupted conversation.

Alone in a quiet restaurant, he asks, "What do you want to talk about?"

"Truthfully?" I ask.

"Yes," he says.

"Nothing. Absolutely nothing."

MAKE MOMMA HAPPY

The following is a test. It contains one very simple question for kids:

Guys and gals, when your mother inquires as to why you haven't (choose one): done your routine household chores, completed your homework, or practiced your flute/piano/ clarinet/drums/violin, what is the response she most desperately wants to hear?

Does your mom want to hear you say, "I didn't have time"?

Think it over carefully. Do you honestly believe that a woman, whose day starts long before yours and lasts several hours after you're snuggled in bed sawing logs, is going to buy the line that you didn't have time?

Probably not.

Try this one. Do you think, when your mom inquires as to your procrastination, forgetfulness, and lack of planning, that she wants to hear you say, "I'll work at it"?

You're getting warmer, kids, but consider this. How would that same answer fly coming from your mom?

Let's say, hypothetically, that you are out of clean underwear because your mom didn't have time to do the laundry. Was your mom blowing time zipping around the neighborhood on her in-line skates, having a gabfest with friends, and playing computer games? Doubtful, but that is an investigation to pursue at another time.

The point is, you are up against the clock trying to get ready for school. You are fishing through piles of rumpled, smelly, dirty clothes and politely ask if she might be running through a load or two of laundry soon. Your mom stands there with a pathetic hound-dog look on her face, shoulders slumped, and says in her most boring monotone voice, "I'll work at it."

That's not exactly a response brimming with promise, now, is it? Maybe you'll have clean underwear tomorrow, maybe not. Maybe she will throw in a load of white clothes or maybe she'll just play Nintendo.

Let's say you sit down to dinner. Plates, glasses, and silverware are on the table. Suddenly, you make the astute observation that there is no food. Your mom shrugs and says, "I'll work at it."

Not real filling, is it? Maybe she'll have a hot meal fixed tomorrow night. Maybe not.

"I'll work at it" is pretty iffy, but it is definitely getting warmer than "I don't have time."

How about this option? Do you think that when your mom inquires as to why the yard has not been mowed, or the dog taken for a walk, she wants to hear you say, "I'll make time"?

Guys and gals, if you chose "I'll make time" as the answer a mother most wants to hear, you are hot, very, very hot. YOUNG PEOPLE, YOU ARE ON FIRE!!!!

Yes! Your mother will be one happy woman when she hears that you will take charge of your time, your universe, your homework, your dental hygiene, and your smelly socks!

"I'll make time" is the answer that will make your mother's heart pound with pride. It is the answer that will make her honk the horn at major intersections and climb to the rooftop to shout to the world that you are her beloved offspring.

Any mother would go wild upon hearing such a positive, go-getter, can-do answer brimming with conviction, optimism, and certainty. With a heartwarming, fabulous answer like that, there's no predicting what might happen next.

Who knows, mom might get so excited that she throws in a load of white clothes and thaws out a pound of ground beef for dinner.

BERRY DANGEROUS

Hard to believe that, only two hours ago, a chunk of frozen fruit almost caused me to maim a man.

Not just any man—the one I love, my husband, the father of our three children. I nearly went for his jugular, all because of an angel food cake and strawberry topping.

What prompted the near attack?

Hard to say exactly. The storm had been brewing all day, stirred by small currents and a prevailing high-pressure system. The thundercloud definitely began escalating, though, with that little question many men routinely pop around six o'clock: "How was your day?"

That sounds easy to answer. But how does a woman summarize, in the time it takes her husband to loosen his tie and open the fridge, events that have propelled her to the brink of lunacy?

"My day? Fine."

What a lie. My day had been like fingernails on a chalkboard.

A semi nearly killed me about 8 A.M. (Okay, a small foreign truck made an extremely abrupt lane change without signaling when I was driving the grade school car pool. But if he'd had a "HOW'S MY DRIVING? CALL 1-800 PEA BRAIN" bumper sticker, I'd still be on the phone leaving a nasty message.)

Shortly before 9 A.M. the dryer vent broke away from the wall and spewed lint all over the kitchen. Breathing in that room was like inhaling baby powder. After folding clothes and ironing, I raced our oldest child to physical therapy, where I spent ninety minutes trying to look calm and relaxed while I watched a therapist twist my kid's leg into a pretzel.

I finally retrieved my morning cup of tea from the microwave at 2 P.M.—right before the plumber arrived to fix the bathtub faucets we had been hoping would heal themselves. He cut a big hole in the wallboard and set off the smoke detectors with his blowtorch. He then all but stuck a .357 Magnum in my back as he wrote out a bill for $250 for forty-five minutes of work.

How was my day?

Fine, just fine.

Actually, the best part of the day had been a quick trip to the grocery store, where I spied an angel food cake. It was irresistible. That cake was everything this day was not—airy, light, and still able to stand upright after 4 P.M. I snagged it and picked up a box of frozen strawberries for accompaniment. They'd be a cheery pick-me-up to an otherwise dismal day.

Dinner wasn't exactly quality time. We were up against a 6:45 P.M. softball game. When I served the cake and berries, one of the kids announced a great idea for a party game. She put her hands behind her back, hunched over, and began to snarf her cake like a dog. Disgusting. I was about to say so, too, at a rather elevated pitch, when my husband asked, "Why are these strawberries frozen?"

You can understand why I considered lunging at him.

I could see the newspaper clipping now: "A man was fatally injured in a fruity melee at the dinner table after inquiring about frozen strawberries. He is survived by a crabby wife, three kids, and a huge, sticky mess in the kitchen."

It's a wonder reports like that don't fill the media daily. "Coming up after *Prime Time Live:* a mechanical engineer accidentally impaled on chopsticks after commenting on the amount of garlic in the stir-fry. Stay tuned, recipe at eleven."

In the interest of stronger marriages everywhere, I offer Communication Tip Number 14 to husbands: When you ask your wife how her day was and she says "fine" without making eye contact, she has just issued the internationally recognized female distress signal. Proceed with extreme caution. Whatever you do, do not criticize any of the food on the table. Just keep your head down, eat, and pray that tomorrow will be better.

TO SWITCH OR NOT TO SWITCH

I never thought of myself as much of a gambler until these phone company battles started heating up. I'm not saying I have a problem of the magnitude Pete Rose had, but it is getting harder and harder to walk away from a good phone wager.

The first time I switched carriers, I was lured by lower rates and a mere $20. Naturally, as soon as my original carrier got the bad news, they called. Actually, a guy named Bob called. He sounded sincerely devastated that, after seven years of faithful service, I would start line hopping. I felt so dirty. Bob begged me to come back and offered me a $30 credit toward my next bill. I took it faster than you could say "speed dial."

Word got out among the phone companies that I was a woman who played fast and loose. Next thing I knew, my number was spread around like graffiti on a restroom wall. There was a time I used to hang up on them, day or night. If

151

they called at dinner, I'd ask for their home number and promise to call them back when they were eating. Now the phone rings and I lunge at it in hopes there will be a phone rep on the other end with higher stakes and bigger thrills, something more than ten cents a minute and free holiday calls.

Truthfully, I suppose it's partly about attention. I can't remember the last time I was pursued like this. A crazy beagle chased me a year ago when I was power walking, but even that doesn't come close to the intense pursuit of the phone companies.

Mike called on Thursday from AT&T. If I'd switch, he'd give me a $20 gift certificate to Bass Pro Shop and $60 off my first month's bill.

"Sorry, Mike, but right now I have a very good relationship with MCI."

"I understand," he said, "but I hope we can still be friends. Mind if I call from time to time?"

What Mike doesn't know is that John also calls from AT&T, on Fridays. John has a jealous streak. If I trash talk MCI a little bit, John sweetens the AT&T deal Mike made me the day before. Of course, I always say I want a little time to think about it before doing something I could regret.

On the first Tuesday of the month, Todd calls from Sprint. This month he was offering a $40 credit toward my first month's bill and $60 worth of checks from Checks By Mail. I would be able to choose the design of my liking— seashore scenes, clowns, wildlife, collectible cars, or floral prints. That's Todd, always dangling a little token of thoughtfulness.

If I had played like a high roller and made all the right moves at the right time, I could now be holding $2,000 in cash, have at least $900 in savings on the phone bills, personalized checks, free personal financial software, and a new tackle box.

152

Of course, I'm not holding anywhere near all that. Once they started talking free mailing labels that coordinate *with* the personalized checks, I knew this game was too rich for my blood. I decided to settle down and quit while I still could. I'm no longer the phone customer whose loyalties can be bought, flitting from one enticing offer to another.

I've been with the same company for six hours now.

MY MOTHER'S VOICE

Not once have I complained to our dentist that Howard Stern transmits radio waves through my fillings. Nor have I ever gone out on a limb with Shirley MacLaine and experienced Aztecs inhabiting my body. But lately, with increasing frequency, I hear the voice of my mother, who lives five hundred miles away, coming out of my own mouth.

I'll be droning on about responsibilities, privileges, and spoons in the garbage disposal when I'm jolted by the realization that the section of my brain programmed to deliver maternal wisdom is shared by my mom. It's somewhat deflating to realize this is not original stuff that I deliver to the kids. It's used material, generations old.

I heard Mom's voice in mine again last week while I held a sobbing child. As one of my daughters cried with an acute awareness that the future is filled with unknowns and uncertainties, my heart ached, too.

But misty-eyed adults are small comfort to sobbing children, so I began to force out some worn words of reassurance. As the words tumbled forth, they resounded with a familiar echo.

I remembered hearing the likes of them from my mother when I lay on a stretcher in a hospital emergency room with broken vertebrae after a car wreck. I don't remember her specific words—just the voice and the tone. The warm inflection, the steady pace of the words, and the presence of a protective mother all synthesized into a message of hope for a scared kid.

Despite pleasant memories of my mother's voice, this is not to imply she was a double for Donna Reed seven days a week. Au contraire. She could stretch vocal chords with the best of them.

Show me a woman who claims she has NEVER raised her voice at her children and I'll show you next week's cover of the *National Inquirer*—"Clinically Dead Mother of Four Never Yells at Kids."

The challenge to the living is how to harness this awesome weapon known as the tongue that can bring immense comfort or inflict cruel devastation.

The power of a mother's voice rings far into the future. I wonder what composite memory my children will hold of my voice? As Stormin' Norman on the battlefield or Roseanne in a hormonal churn? Will they remember the laughing more than the lecturing? Will our conversations be remembered as relaxed, or hurried and on edge, struggling to squeeze in a few minutes of "quality time"?

Will they remember me talking to them from behind the pages of *Newsweek,* or face-to-face? Will they remember hearing words of love and acceptance far more often than words of disappointment and reprimand?

One thing I am positive of is this: On bad days I'd be better off not talking at all. Word-free. Why not. I'm nearly sugar-free, salt-free, and hydofluorocarbon-free now. I think it's time to seriously examine the merits of humming.

Instead of the weekly lecture insisting the health department really can close down a dirty bedroom if they want to, I'm pondering just pounding on the kitchen table and humming "Wipe Out." Humming "Rubber Ducky" could replace my fourteen-point checklist itemizing the "Cultural Advantages to Smelling Fresh."

Think of it. Everyone knows people who hum appear happy, at peace with the world, and possibly one bottle shy of a full six-pack.

So if it's a choice between being remembered as a hard-edged scolding nag, or as a slightly eccentric habitual hummer—well, I'd rather be remembered as having a song in my heart.

SO SORRY

For a nanosecond, I seriously considered lunging over the counter, grabbing that overgrown adolescent by his skinny tie, and tightening it eighteen inches for him. I regained my senses and realized that at 5'2" there was no way I could clear a 4'6" counter. At least not in a skirt.

In a loud, exasperated, snotty voice, the young video store clerk sneered, "My records show an overdue charge dated last Friday on your video card from a rental of *The Care Bears Movie*. It also shows you purchased three boxes of Jubilees that day."

"And, sir, I'm telling you that is impossible because: one, everybody at our house hopes that no-plot cast of furball Care Bears will either appear on the endangered species list—or permanently hibernate; and two, I would never buy candy here that I could get at half the cost at the grocery store."

"Well, if you didn't check it out, your husband probably did."

"I don't think so. He worked that night. Plus his tastes are a little more sophisticated than Care Bears. He prefers Road Runner."

The clerk advised me that the people at video central had very special computers that *never* make errors and *never* let clerks make errors either. He finished with, "Would you like to pay the outstanding charges now?"

Take a guess, Bucky!

I left seething. It wasn't just that this kid had yelled at me and humiliated me in front of a line of strangers. He falsely accused me and branded me a liar. And I had no defense. No recourse. No power.

Licking my wound on the walk home, I realized what had happened to me that afternoon has happened to my children. Only, I'm the one that has done it to them. It was a good reminder of how it feels to stand off against someone who seemingly holds all the cards, has all the answers, and possesses all the power.

There have been times I've executed justice faster than a two-year-old can knock over a glass of ice water at a cloth-napkin restaurant. Then, as pieces of the puzzle I didn't even know were missing appeared, everything changed. All that's left to do is to humbly tuck my tail between my legs and say I'm sorry.

Sounds simple. But apologizing is about as natural to most adults as paying income taxes with a smile. And that's too bad, because there's a lot of power that can be unleashed in those simple words, "I'm sorry." Apologizing can sweeten a sour relationship, cool a flash-point temper, or restore a child's self-esteem. As I watch my own kids try to mend fences, I am uncomfortably aware that their behavior is often patterned after mine.

There's the halfhearted apology that's uttered while they attempt to vibrate the drywall from the foundation by stomping away with the force of a sumo wrestler. "SAAAAAW-ry," they snarl with a hung head and curled lip. Definitely not the real thing.

They are master manipulators as they retort with a chipper, "I'm sorry," followed by a quick, but equally insincere, "I love you!"

There's the drama queen who can turn the waterworks on full blast and hurl herself into a chair, sobbing that she is worthless and inept. The chest heaves in and out, arms flail, and hands dramatically sweep hair out of the eyes. With an audience, the show runs about three minutes; without spectators it's twenty seconds tops. It's Emmy-winning stuff, but that does not mask the fact that no apology is included in the theatrics.

A close second is the "I'm-sorrier-than-you-are" routine.

"I'm sorry."

"No, I'M sorry!"

"Oh yeah, well I'm sorry about your face."

"Yeah? Well I'm sorry you were born *#@$%&*&%$ ..."

The apology escalates rapidly, requiring immediate adult intervention and occasional first aid.

But once in awhile there is the genuine, "I'm sorry. I was wrong. Will you forgive me?"

It's hard to teach kids how to apologize. Maybe that's because a sincere apology is a lot more than parroting some trite memorized words.

I went back to the video store and explained my situation to another young clerk with a skinny tie. He listened, punched a few computer keys, and explained that my card had not cleared the computer before the person behind me checked out his movie.

He looked me straight in the eye and said, "I'm really sorry." To back it up, he gave me a credit for future video rentals. Now that's an apology. I felt so good, I almost felt bad about slandering the Care Bears.

What can I say? I'm sorry.

PLEASE DON'T CALL IT NAGGING

The verdict is in on nagging. There's no gentle way to break it to you fellas (and pardon me if I sound a little giddy here), but it turns out that a researcher at Ohio State University found that most naggers tend to be female because women have more to nag about, not because of their gender.

Liberation from the cruel stereotype of a nagging shrew is cause for celebration. I can't begin to tell you what this burden has been. Hello? Are you listening? Well, let me start over. I know I'm repeating myself, but I wouldn't have to repeat myself if someone would acknowledge me once in awhile when I am talking.

Anyway, you can't imagine what it is like to have your loving, subtle suggestions and caring, gentle nudging callously labeled as nagging.

Nagging is such an unpleasant word, which is why I have always preferred to call what I do "repetitive reminding." This researcher fella calls it "demanding." He observed married couples and found a problem pattern of demand-withdraw communication. Most often, women demand and men withdraw. Women make more frequent demands than men because women work from a very long list of concerns: child care, cleaning, cooking, shopping, and household chores. Men make fewer demands because, according to the study, they work from a very short list: sex.

I think we all know how this demand-withdraw pattern goes. A wife sweetly asks if her husband would pretty please help put out a raging grease fire on the stove in the kitchen because she has one hand busy changing diapers on the twins and the other hand running the vacuum sweeper. He motions with his hand for her to step aside—because she is blocking the final quarter of a playoff game. The man withdraws, believing a significant chunk of power in the marital relationship is at stake, namely the remote control and a comfortable spot on the sofa.

Part of the problem is that men and women have profoundly different definitions when it comes to nagging. Most women claim they don't nag. They may remind men about things that need to be done (get the taxes done, get the taxes done, get the taxes done), but they don't nag. Now to hear a man tell it, a woman doesn't even need to talk to nag.

I coincidentally clear my throat at the precise moment my husband is drowning two lettuce leaves in a bottle of ranch salad dressing and I am nagging about cholesterol. Did I open my mouth? Did I utter a syllable? I did not.

I instinctively slam my foot through the floor of the passenger side of the van when my husband is tailgating a semi-trailer and I'm nagging. Did I criticize? Did I rant and rave? I did not. I may have taken down my husband's license number, whipped out a cell phone, and reported him to a state trooper, but I did not nag.

I happen to mention a leaky bathroom faucet a few dozen times, post nine reminders about the faucet on the refrigerator door, and stuff a tube of caulk under his pillow and he says I'm nagging. I am not nagging; I am helping.

We women may repeat ourselves occasionally (you need more exercise, you need more exercise, you need more exercise) or reiterate a point sixty-six times in one evening, but we do not nag. We just work from a very long list of demands.

IF IT WALKS LIKE A CRAB AND TALKS LIKE A CRAB

If a kid comes home from a slumber party and says she's not tired, she's not tired. The fact that she bumps into walls, trips over her own two feet, and slumps at the bottom of the stairs because she's too weak to climb them is irrelevant. The fact that she spent the night with five friends who were running, screaming, jumping, pillow fighting, and doing gymnastics until four in the morning is immaterial. And please, ignore those dark bags under her eyes that are the size of mail pouches once carried by riders for the Pony Express.

What's more, if the kid says she doesn't feel sick, she doesn't feel sick. Forget the fact that in your eyes she looks like the poster child for the Black Plague. Forget the fact that in the previous twelve hours she gorged herself on popcorn, ice cream, soda pop, hot chocolate, and doughnuts. Those foods don't make a kid sick.

She'll tell you what makes a kid sick—brussel sprouts and beets. Now those are foods that will send a kid running for the bathroom with her hands over her mouth. But not pizza bagels, nachos, and root beer floats. Those are the three food groups as nature intended them.

And if the kid says she's not crabby, she's not crabby. Get off her back. As a matter of fact, it might be a good idea to get away from her front and side, too. And for the sake of world peace, don't argue with her about whether the storm door did or did not deliberately smack her in the rear end when she walked in the house. And please, don't be lured into the no-win debate about whether the company that made the shoestrings in her tennis shoes too long is run by a bunch of jerks.

If the kid says she's not tired, she's not sick, and she's not crabby, that should put an end to the discussion. The kid ought to know how she feels, right?

So why is the kid who says she is not tired, not crabby, and not sick, now sleeping? Soundly. Very soundly. She's making Z's like Rip van Winkle. Sawing logs so hard that a forty-pack mule train passing directly over the sofa where she rests would not cause her to shift, stir, or twitch the slightest.

The child who is not tired has been sleeping for half an hour, an hour, two hours. Three hours later and the child who is not tired is still in slumberland in the family room, a resting spot that bears all the tranquility of LaGuardia Airport the day before Christmas. She has slept through heavy volume pedestrian traffic, Sci-Fi theater blasting on the tube, the phone ringing, the microwave beeping, and a souped-up

'72 Mustang without a muffler roaring up and down the street.

The kid who is not tired has slept through lunch and dinner and is fast approaching bedtime. She has slept six consecutive hours and still counting.

Naturally, when she wakes, it will be a temptation to ask how her nap was. Of course, it also would be obtuse to ask such a question. Why would anybody take a nap when they weren't tired, sick, or crabby in the first place?

11

Holiday **HUSTLE**

A broadcaster reported that, over the Christmas holidays, the average person gains about seven pounds. He sounded positively shocked. Obviously, he didn't know the holidays technically start with Halloween.

Most moms feel duty bound to do their trick-or-treaters a big favor and help eat all the candy—you know, save their teeth, insure stable blood sugar levels. This selfless task continues through several weeks and at least two pounds. No sooner has the last miniature candy bar been devoured and your sister-in-law calls asking you to try a new pumpkin pie recipe with a graham cracker crust and walnut topping, to see if she should bring it for Thanksgiving dinner (add one more pound). Then there's the Thanksgiving feast itself (add one pound), which comes with the mandatory pretesting, sampling, and snacking (add two pounds) that goes on day and night in the kitchen so weary cooks can keep their energy up.

Then there are the leftovers (add two pounds). By the time the last turkey sandwich disappears, we are into early December. Early December means commencement of the cookie baking season (add two pounds), which takes us right up to the eleven-pound mark with still two weeks to go until Christmas.

162

I was shocked by the radio report, too. Seven pounds was clearly an underestimate.

HOW DO I LOVE THEE?

Valentine's Day confronts married women with an agonizing dilemma:. Do you buy the oversized, embossed, elegant "To My Husband" Valentine card that plays "It Had to Be You" for $6.95? Or do you shop from the bottom of the rack and buy the plain, generic "To the One I Love" for only $1.35 so you'll have enough cash left over for two gallons of milk?

When you're first married, there is no choice. You buy from the top of the rack—romantic cards with pop-ups, a dusting of glitter, and frosted overlay sheets. That's because when you are first married, love is happy-ever-after fairy tales, Hallmark, and Laura Ashley all rolled into one.

When you are newlyweds, love is a dozen long-stemmed roses from the florist, dinner by candlelight, and silky lingerie. Twenty-one years, one mortgage, two car payments, and three kids later, love is six pink carnations from the grocery store, carry-out pizza, and sleeping in an over-sized T-shirt that says "Go Ask Your Dad."

Love changes over time. It's still there, it just expresses itself in a different form. At least that's what I told myself the year I received a large gift box containing a paper cutter. He's a practical romantic, I said. If a safety-guard between your thumb and the edge of an eighteen-inch razor-sharp blade doesn't say love, I don't know what does.

Unless, of course, it would be a brand-new cobalt blue twelve-inch T-fal skillet with ovenproof handle. That's not love, you say? Sure it is. They *claim* old skillets with flaking Teflon chips don't pose a health hazard, but only a hopelessly-in-love husband would be unwilling to take a chance.

In the same manner, only a starry-eyed wife would give her husband a personal and intimate gift like a bright red Sears Craftsman twelve-foot tree pruner. Obviously, she's so crazy in love with him, she can't stand to watch him teeter on an old rickety ladder lunging at those just-out-of-reach branches.

Sometimes, love is when he gases the car up in the dead of winter and cleans the back windshield. Sometimes, love is when she stops at the dry cleaners for his jacket because he doesn't have time.

Other times, love is having the alarm go off and your spouse offering to hit the shower first so you can have ten extra minutes of shut-eye.

Love is when your husband does not comment on the fact that you are still fighting to lose those last few pounds of "baby weight" and the "baby" is now thirteen years old.

Love is when he insists on driving you to the airport, drives all the way back to his office, gets out of the car, notices a package you meant to take with you, gets back in the car, drives back to the airport, parks the car, finds your departure gate, hustles through the terminal, and delivers the package two minutes before you board your plane.

Love is when you set an overflowing trash can in the middle of the kitchen floor and he takes it out and dumps it instead of jumping over it like a high hurdle.

Love is when the one human being on this earth who knows your good side and bad, your erratic mood swings, oddities, and peculiarities better than any other, looks you in the eyes and says if he had it to do over again, he would— and you believe he really means it.

THE PERFECT MOTHER'S DAY

I know this is a terrible breach of etiquette. I only hope Miss Manners is busy laundering a pair of white gloves while I make this true confession: I would like to script my own Mother's Day celebration this year. That's right, I'd like to make the plans celebrating me, myself.

The trouble is, I'm not exactly sure what I want.

I have a friend who knows what she wants. She says her perfect Mother's Day would be an extension of the ending of the old *Queen for a Day* program. That's where the winner, the woman with the saddest tale of woe, was seated on a throne, adorned with a crown, presented with a dozen roses, and cloaked in a red cape. Then the entire audience, including the other two losing contestants, acknowledged the winner's survival skills, endurance, and perseverance with round after round of thunderous applause.

I don't need anything quite that grandiose, but there are a few small amenities that would make for a wonderful day.

For starters—and I may well stand alone on this one—I'd scrap breakfast in bed. It's a wonderful gesture, but it makes me feel like I'm in the hospital. Toast crumbs in the rumpled sheets often cause me to think the next event on the agenda will be an IV in the crook of my arm.

I'd be perfectly content to come downstairs to a lace cloth on the breakfast table, some lilies of the valley plucked from the yard, an open window, 72-degree temperatures, a soft breeze, brand-name orange juice, and a huge, sticky pecan roll.

Am I going too fast?

Chirping birds and refrains from Strauss waltzes are the only sounds I'd like to hear on Mother's Day. I'd like a complete cessation of sibling fighting, complaining, and tattling. In my most daring dreams I envision two uninterrupted hours on the sofa with a good book and an hour on the patio without a single softball whizzing by my head.

As for visual delights, I'd like to see my children freshly scrubbed and dressed in their finest. I'd like the house picked up all day, no book bags on the kitchen floor, no tennis shoes on the stairs, and no wet dishtowels slung across the kitchen faucet.

I'd also like to be banned from the kitchen for twenty-four hours. Go ahead, get forceful. Physically restrain me from the sink, stove, and silverware drawer. Block me from the canned goods and shield me from the freezer. Adamantly demand I not tend to a single juice spill, sandwich fiasco, or the wrapping and care of a solitary leftover.

We now come to gifts. Honestly, a handwritten card, a verse, or a poem—anything from the heart that shows my family thinks of me half as fondly as I think of them would be lovely. Of course, if they insisted on purchasing some small token of affection (with their own money) in recognition of my efforts as cook, seamstress, scrub woman, laundress, paramedic, chauffeur, backyard referee, hairstylist, tutor, and counselor, I would graciously accept it.

Above all, however this day takes shape, I would like it to look as though it was planned. I didn't say it *had* to be planned, just give me the illusion that it was planned.

A mother's job description requires her to remember a vast assortment of birthdates, Social Security numbers, and shoe sizes. Which explains why we get a little testy when someone else has 364 days to plan for Mother's Day and they claim they "forgot."

I think that about does it. Well, almost. Perhaps one small round of applause would be rather nice.

WHEN THE ANTS GO MARCHING IN

The ants arrived three weeks ago and promptly erected a command post on the east side of the house. Their perennial task has gone according to plan as platoon after platoon has marched in formation, back and forth and over and under the burgeoning peony buds.

Ants aren't the only ones with a tradition of fretting over the peonies: My mother and grandmother did it for years. Peonies predictably came under scrutiny in the month of May. Would the spring rains beat them down? Would they be ready in time? Would the blooms be too far along, wilted and browning around the edges? Or would they still be curled in a ball, needing to be forced open in warm water?

The enormous pink, red, and white ruffled peonies were Midwestern essentials to Decoration Day. South of the Mason-Dixon line, it was magnolia blossoms that were used on the first Decoration Day more than a century ago.

On April 25, 1866, four young women paid a visit to a cemetery outside Columbus, Mississippi, to tend the graves of loved ones fallen in the Battle of Shiloh. After decorating the Confederate graves, the women walked to a small plot where forty Union soldiers were buried. They tenderly scattered Southern magnolia blossoms on the graves of Northern soldiers.

In 1868, General John A. Logan, commander-in-chief of a veterans group called the Grand Army of the Republic, declared May 30 as Decoration Day. He chose that date because flowers used to decorate graves would be in bloom all across the country.

At the end of the nineteenth century, Decoration Day, or Memorial Day as it is now known, was celebrated with greater fanfare than Independence Day.

Today, Memorial Day is observed over a three-day weekend packed with race festivities, retail sales, cookouts, and opening day at the pool. But sometime between Friday afternoon and Tuesday morning, it is still a time to remember loved ones who have preceded us in death. In particular, it is a time to reflect upon members of the armed forces who gave their lives in service to our country.

Like many people my age, I have never experienced the agony of losing an immediate family member to battle. I will

167

not be among those cutting bouquets of peonies to decorate the grave of a soldier who was once my beloved husband, son, brother, or father. But I will fly the flag and pause to remember.

Old Glory is a reminder of the uncle I never met, my brother's namesake. He was a nineteen-year-old Nebraska farm boy killed on June 8, 1945, while serving in the U.S. Infantry in Mindanao, Philippines.

My father was being inducted at Fort Leavenworth, Kansas, when he learned of his brother's death. He was granted a three-day leave to return home to be with his grieving family.

Dad remembers watching his father lie on the sofa in a state of shock and sorrow. It was a scene of unbearable mourning that has been repeated countless times over the years as telegrams and officers in dress uniforms have delivered the news families hoped never to receive.

The flag's red stripes are a stark reminder of the blood shed by 1.1 million soldiers over the course of our nation's history. Whether inductees or volunteers, serving out of duty or love for country, they paid the high price that freedom sometimes demands. We best pay them homage today by honoring their memory and by treasuring their legacy, the costly gifts of liberty and freedom.

CHRISTMAS IN JULY

My mom just called to say that only minutes ago she finished wrapping the last Christmas gift. I looked out the window. The leaves on the maple trees are still green and clinging to the branches. The air conditioner is running full-blast and the kids are wearing shorts.

My mom hails from the gene pool that produces the Hyper-Efficient. She is well-organized, extremely productive, and continually thirty-five minutes ahead of schedule.

You know these people. They address the envelopes for their Christmas cards in early October and are first in line when the holiday stamps go on sale at Halloween. By election day, they're putting finishing touches on the cute handmade gifts for the kids' teachers, the mail carrier, and the trash man.

Their annual Christmas family photo was shot on a Monday in July, processed on Tuesday, and labeled with names, ages, and stellar accomplishments on Wednesday. Everyone in the picture has been coordinated for style. They are all wearing denim with a splash of red—even the parakeet.

These are the same people who never exceed three thousand miles before an oil change. On the first of every month they check the batteries in their smoke alarms and update their alphabetized list of most frequently called phone numbers.

You see these people all the time. They are the ones surgically attached to bulging personal organizers twice the size of *War and Peace*. The concepts of last-minute, unfinished, and mañana do not exist in their repertoire.

Most highly organized people, in addition to ingesting toxic amounts of caffeine, are also compulsive list makers. There's something magic about their lists. They write an item down on a scrap of paper and one week later it has been accomplished. I write something on a scrap of paper and one week later the list is still lying by the microwave, but is now spattered with grease stains, spaghetti sauce, and several coffee grounds.

I have sporadic success with list making. My major downfall is not being able to factor in small interruptions like working, eating, and sleeping.

One of the best ways to gauge how well organized you are is by how often you run out of toilet paper. That never happens in a master planner's home. They also never have to turn off the mixer in the middle of a baking project and race to the store for a missing ingredient.

I admire highly organized people, especially the ones who are fully prepared to celebrate Christmas before the autumnal equinox. But I worry that they miss out on a significant portion of the holiday festivities like the frantic shopping trips and parking lot roulette.

Not to worry, the master planners claim. They would much rather be at home during the month of December, lounging in front of a roaring fire, sipping on a mug of hot chocolate. Besides, what better time than December to begin planning your Fourth of July picnic?

We definitely need more master planners and super organizers in the world today. We just don't need them reminding the rest of us how behind schedule we are.

MARY WITH THE DARK BLUE NOSE

The house has been decorated for two weeks and *Midwest Living* magazine still hasn't stopped by to register us for their holiday Tour of Homes. Maybe they're hung up on the fact that a number of our decorations look more like flea market finds than Hallmark keepsakes.

We still have the nativity figures we purchased the first year we were married. We bought Mary, Joseph, and the baby Jesus on our lunch hour at a downtown dime store for ninety-nine cents each. Years of handling by little people have been far harder on Mary and Joseph than the trip to Bethlehem. Joseph's nose is missing and the paint on Mary's hands and face has worn away, revealing a blue undercoating. They are pretty pathetic looking, and maybe I'm just being superstitious, but I don't feel right about tossing the holy family into the trash. So, the weathered figurines sit adjacent to a table hosting a small greenery arrangement.

It is a small tabletop decoration, a chestnut brown basket filled with evergreens, lifelike holly berries, and a big red ribbon. It is fifteen years old and looks like it. I should toss it, but my Aunt Jean had a florist deliver it when I was expecting our first child and battling morning sickness around the clock. I was so sick that I watered that perky little arrangement for six days before I realized that it was artificial. It makes a dynamic visual aid to my "The Sacrifices I've Made For You" lecture.

Our stockings have been hung by the chimney with care, but they're looking a little worse for the wear. Last year I considered buying some beautiful needlepoint stockings at an after-Christmas sale, but put them back. Our handmade stockings aren't exactly works of art, but they are from my craft days when the kids were only four, two, and two months old. Those stockings are a tribute to what a little colored felt, green and red sequins, and a bottle of craft glue can do to help keep your mental health intact.

How did we sink to this sad state of decor? Well, Christmas decorations aren't like chipped cups and cracked plates. There are some things you just don't toss. Believe me, I've tried.

When no one was looking, I recently pitched a dilapidated paper star ornament with someone's preschool picture glued to the center. Moments later, I envisioned the trash bag splitting open at the curb, a strong gust of wind catching the paper star and blowing it directly into the path of my child walking home from school. She would pick it up, bring it inside, and ask, "How'd this get outside, Mom?"

It was back on the tree in thirty seconds. It hangs surrounded by some lovely, newer decorations. In fact, if we weeded out the ragged decorations, the remaining goods wouldn't look half bad. The catch is, the decorations that came wrapped in department store tissue paper are far less heartwarming than the ones that came wrapped in sticky hands and memories.

On the surface, the reindeer with pipe cleaner antlers and the cotton ball sheep missing one twig leg aren't much to look at. They require a special eye able to look beneath the surface—the same sort of eye able to discern that a baby born in a manger might really be the King of Kings.

OVER THE RIVER

I personally doubt it ever happened. You know, that over the river and through the woods business, where the horse knew the way to carry the sleigh, through white and drifted snow. A pink-cheeked family piled three-deep in a sleigh, all warm and cozy with their wool lap blankets and furry muffs, smiling from ear to ear as they face the prospect of blizzards, exposure, frostbite, and the threat of bobcats, mountain lions, and wolves.

Right. Like family holiday travel would ever be that easy.

Our family excels at making holiday travel complicated. Take our Chicago relations. They're math and science type people who are big planners. They plan and plan and plan because their overriding plan is that all plans are subject to change. Their most recent holiday travel plan is as follows:

They will leave Chicago in two cars on Wednesday afternoon. Car A plans on traveling at 55 mph, leaving after the high school kid arrives home and will make a slight detour off the interstate to pick up another offspring who is in college. Car B plans on leaving Chicago sixty minutes later at 70 mph (speed limits are merely suggestions for other people), headed directly toward the interstate. Or maybe Car B will leave ninety minutes later. Or maybe Car A and Car B will leave at the same time.

In any case, both cars will meet here at midnight. Or a little before. Or a little after. You get the idea.

The Ohio wing of the family does not open a car door or turn an ignition key without final clearance from the

Weather Channel. No travel arrangements are firm until viewing the national temperature chart, wind pattern projections, and a precipitation map tracking sleet, snow, and freezing rain.

If the Weather Trackers learn there is the possibility of light snow in Anchorage, all travel plans will be red flagged. After all, if there's one thing they've learned from the Weather Channel, it's that weather can change very quickly. That Anchorage weather system may be three thousand miles away at 7 A.M., but who's to say where it will be after the next commercial break.

The west of the Mississippi branch of the family we simply refer to as the Minute Men. They keep the gas tank full and leave their shoes pointed toward the garage when they go to bed just in case they should get an invitation during the night. Be it for a wedding, funeral, birth, or cheese and crackers celebrating the vernal equinox, these folks can be ready to go with three changes of clothes, a thermos of hot coffee, and an appropriate hostess gift in a New York minute.

I'm just so delighted to have a house bustling with family and friends for the holidays that I don't care when they come or how they come. Horse-drawn sleigh or coaster wagon, the more the merrier. Even when all the beds are full, two bodies are camped on the sofa, and a couple more are snoozing on the floor, there is always room for more.

I get so carried away with Christmas that I would be tickled pink if a couple of foreigners showed up at the front door on a donkey. They might have to sleep out back in the tool-shed on some loose straw, but they'd be more than welcome.

12

Hang on to HOPE

There are days when the roles of a mother and a drill sergeant are hard to separate. We routinely bark orders, slop hash, do room inspections, and give marching orders. Some nights we slump into bed and wonder if any of it really makes a difference. And then, in the next day or week, something happens. In an unexpected moment, we catch a brief glimpse of something beautiful. We see a child (*our* child!), demonstrating compassion, utilizing good manners, or expressing heartfelt love. And that's all that most of us need to keep going for another six months.

Some of the best advice for mothers has come, ironically, not from a woman, but from a man. He was a man who possessed many of the abilities necessary for mothering. He stayed focused under great duress, was a keen strategist, a remarkable leader, and savvy negotiator. He was Sir Winston Churchill. His best advice every mother should take to heart?

"Never, never, never give up!"

THE BIG MUDDY

It is not by choice that I find myself standing here with muddy water rippling around my knees and thick, cool muck oozing between my toes. The promise of pleasure did not call me to this creek. Duty did. Maternal duty.

I am here swatting away four-pound mosquitoes in order to see the stream that draws my children like moths to a porch light. I've followed them here to see if the creek is safe, to see if the water is deep, and to see, for the love of all creation, what the big attraction is.

An inflatable raft and fly fishing pole in the possession of one teenage boy leads our small procession. The midsection of our outfit consists of his two younger sisters, one of their friends, and an old metal colander for sifting treasures from the stream. I, the self-appointed rear guard, keep a vigilant watch for water snakes, snapping turtles, and legions of leeches.

We traipse about a hundred feet through shallow water bordered on both sides by towering cottonwoods and dense underbrush. As we ease around the bend, the water deepens and the creek widens. A small reef with a crescent moon shoreline beckons to those with sore feet. Mud gives way to sand and a large bed of small, flat stones ideal for skipping across placid pools of water. A few large rocks form a natural seat on which to watch and dry.

Fresh paw prints looking like x-rays of miniature hands abound on this tiny isle. They belong to four-legged masked bandits who venture out at twilight to hunt at the water's edge before ravaging neighborhood garbage cans. Less abundant are the impressions of hooves left by deer, now resting unseen beneath a thick canopy of trees that somehow has managed to stand undisturbed in this pocket of suburbia.

The girls take turns floating in the raft upon a quiet stretch of water. My son baits his line with a Royal Wulff fly and begins to cast. Fishing line arcs gracefully in the sky, dancing free-form in the golden shafts of sunlight.

The silence is broken only by the sounds of nature: water splashing, the chatter of chickadees, and the rustle of leaves. This creek is a world away from the noise of nearby strip malls, the wail of sirens, and the clamor of the television and telephone.

As my eyes slowly adjust, I begin to see more clearly. I see that the water is not so deep as to be dangerous, but deep enough to buoy imagination. They are fly fishing the Salmon River in Idaho, rafting in a Cascade Mountain stream, and resting at an unmarked campsite in the Rockies.

I see the shadows of Lewis and Clark, Tom Sawyer, Huck Finn, and Old Jim. I see school is in session with Mother Nature presiding as Headmistress. She has taught them well on the subjects of snakes, geodes, poison ivy, and catfish.

Looking intently past the dirt and the mud, I can even finally see the big attraction. It rests in the shy blue heron and sunfish dappled with color. I see now why this is a place where children long to come. It is a visit to a beautiful picture postcard sent by the Great Outdoorsman Himself.

IN THE BLINK OF AN EYE

It was a Lartigue moment. A Lartigue moment is similar to a Kodak moment, only cheaper: You save the cost of film and processing.

Jacques-Henri Lartigue's zany family snapshots, which he took as a young lad in France in the early 1900s, have come to be regarded as documentary art. But before the boy ever owned a camera, he tried to be one himself. He believed he could fix a scene firmly in his mind by blinking rapidly three times.

It's not the best substitute for prints or slides, but as one who rarely travels with a camera in tow, I've fallen into the Lartigue moment habit. One of these moments occurred while riding in the car.

My son was furiously punching numbers on a calculator. His hair was styled with sweat and his shoes were caked with mud. He was off in his own zone, wildly hammering at the calculator.

I blinked three times and marveled at how quickly he'd changed from that demanding toddler who would rise before the sun, waddle to the front door, lunge at the doorknob, and scream, "Outside, outside!" Ten years later, he was now a kid who could open the door himself.

"I've got it," he said. "On Tuesday, I'll be exactly four thousand days old, figuring for leap years. Do you want to make me a cake?"

With that, a profound little truth smacked me like Scarlett O'Hara belted Rhett Butler: Those were four thousand finite days of life I'd shared with this boy. That was real time sandwiched between soggy Cheerios and nighttime prayers, an accumulation of years in which the minute hand had swept the face of the clock nearly 5.5 million times.

Then I wondered, if someone had handed him to me as an infant with a four-thousand-day calendar, would I have done things differently? Would I have taken the job of parenting more seriously? Probably so. Would I have set weekly goals, followed developmental charts, and done time-and-motion studies? Probably not.

Even without a strictly charted course, as I view the scales teetering between barbarian and civilized, we are making remarkable progress toward civilized behavior. All three kids recognize the basic shapes of eating utensils, two out of three can go an entire meal without falling off their chairs, and only one still parades seminaked in front of the hall window after a bath.

This domestication process has left me with volumes of Lartigue-type images stored in a photo album in my head:

♦ A four-year-old wearing nothing but a crown of ribbons she received for her birthday, holding the coordinating magic wand while reading her big sister's diary.
♦ A room completely engulfed in talcum powder after a child armed with two tubes of Tinker Bell's finest squeezed them in rapid-fire succession "just for the fun of it."
♦ A young man digging a hole in the backyard in order to bury a plastic bag containing his dress shoes.

I wonder what images the kids have stored in their memory banks. It was a risk, but I asked.

Hands down, the most memorable image for all three kids is the precise instant Dad fell in the creek while fishing. They remember a goofy experiment from four years ago when we had "Upside Down Day" and ate macaroni and cheese for breakfast. One remembers a Tennessee motel by name because it has a pool we let them swim in until 11 P.M.

Not one kid has a single freeze-frame of me reading clever little children's books heavily ladened with moralistic messages. Nor do they hold dear any images of me in lecture mode, rambling on about the importance of attitudes.

Certainly, reading and lecturing are critical parts that contribute to the whole of child-raising, but maybe the old cliché persists because it is true: More is caught than taught. And often, it's in the blink of an eye.

OF LACE, LINENS, AND TEA

The battered card table has been tenderly covered with a Quaker lace tablecloth. Twice. The enormous cloth had hung in such excess on the floor that the hostess flipped it back over the table a second time. And then a third. It is doubtful the guests would notice a few gentle ripples in the thick layers of cloth.

Place settings have been arranged with meticulous care. The hostess has tried numerous creative arrangements: crystal goblets to the side of the ruby red luncheon plates, crystal goblets at the top right of the ruby red luncheon plates, and crystal goblets upside down in the dead center of the ruby red luncheon plates. Top right it would be. Cloth napkins have been rolled, twisted, and stuffed into the goblets, reportedly resembling roses to anyone with an ounce of imagination.

No knives, forks, or spoons accompany the place settings. Fingers are the order of the day. Fingers will work well with the hard candy mints (red and white striped, wrapped in cellophane) scattered randomly across the table in a carefree postmodern sort of way. Name cards have been written in cursive with a wide-tip felt marker on scraps of tangerine orange poster board.

The place settings ring the center attraction—a pedestal cake plate boasting a spectacular display of cookies. The hostess has forever been enamored with the grocery store bakery and its ability to produce cookies in soft pastel colors and uniform shapes. She has never noticed their hardwood flavor and petrified icing. Cucumber sandwiches have been politely declined. No thank you, the hostess said. But was there any beef jerky in the house?

As for tea, chamomile, mint, or earl grey, the response is "Blechh!" Sparkling white grape juice will be the beverage of choice.

This is a tea for discriminating palates, a tea less rambunctious than the Boston Tea Party, but a few notches shy of the Queen's standards. This will be a tea by the people, for the people, short people yet in grade school who still occasionally play with dolls.

Guests are now arriving in a most unusual fashion. They are using the sidewalk leading to the front door and ringing the bell. Strange behavior for a group that normally appears on in-line skates, tears across the backyard at 40 mph, or barrels in through the kitchen after scrambling over trash bags in the garage.

Their appearance is unusual as well. One guest has shed her trademark ponytail for loose curls and a soft blue satin ribbon. Still another guest, legendary for her ability to hide both eyes with a single jerk of her bangs, has both peepers in full view and is wearing a bonnet identical to the one worn by her doll.

If their arrival and appearances have not been alarming enough, stranger still are their voices. They are being exercised at normal conversational levels. "Please. Thank you. Pardon me. You first. Shall we?"

Shall?

Who are these girls? Are these the same girls who shout at one another from two blocks away because it is faster than using the phone? Are these the same girls who hang upside down from the swing set until their faces turn purple? Are these the same girls who can steal second and slide into third?

Indeed they are. What is unfolding are the amazing powers of tea. It is the mystery of white lace and pretty dishes. Such frills can be potent, able to transform urchins willing to wrestle for the last handful of popcorn into little ladies worthy of pillbox hats, white kid gloves, and Jackie O. pearls.

Maybe we should do tea more often.

BRIDGING THE GAP

He looked a little out of place, not unlike the chair he was sitting on, brown vinyl with sturdy chrome legs. The chair, now in the living room, really belonged with five others just like it still gathered around the blond-laminate-topped table in the kitchen.

Shortly before Thanksgiving he had moved the chair in here for his wife. She'd been having difficulty getting out of her big upholstered chair, with it's soft padded back, thick cushion, and large rolled arms.

It was one of the many accommodations that people in their eighties routinely make. Of course, no change, however small, is simple. As the kitchen chair moved to the living room, the living room chair then moved to the front room.

In this house, the front room is where all items in transit or with uncertain futures tend to congregate. It's an eclectic assortment that includes an office desk, a children's table and chair set, a stationary bicycle, and stacks of books and magazines, most of which have been waiting years for permanent assignments.

The brown vinyl chair, however, has received a very specific assignment. It serves as anchor to the living room control center. The control center, with its invisible boundaries, measures about four feet square. Every necessity is within arm's reach:

To the right of the chair, on a two-tiered end table are a lamp, a radio, a booklet of inspirational poetry, tissues, eye drops, and old greeting cards from special friends.

To the left of the chair, on a small, low, round table, sit the telephone, a list of frequently called numbers, the remote control, and *TV Guide.*

Perhaps it was because he wasn't utilizing any of the control center's many offerings that his presence caught my eye. He was dressed for the falling snow outside, wearing winter boots, a heavy flannel shirt, and old pants. But he made no effort to move. Something across the room commanded his full attention.

"What is that?" he finally asked.

"This?" said the thirteen-year-old boy.

"Show it to me."

"Sure."

The boy walked across the room, still playing a hand-held computer game. His white-haired grandfather rose from the brown chair, put his arm around the boy's shoulders, and asked for a demonstration.

"It's an electronic game with a digital display. You try to get from one level to the next; these coins represent chances. The "A" button moves you vertically and the "B" button . . . well, it's like an arcade game."

Arcade game. Finally, a concept someone over eighty could relate to. But the last time his grandpa was in an arcade was more than forty years ago, when pinball machines with levers and bells were standard fare.

Nonetheless, Grandpa listened intently.

The boy continued playing, explaining the game action and tilting the screen so his grandpa could get a better look. And look he did—he looked at the boy's hair with its thick waves. He looked at the boy's changing facial features and darkening eyebrows. He ran his hand up and down the boy's arm as though to warm him and squeezed his shoulder.

Meanwhile, the boy continued narrating the on-screen action. He'd had the game for six months, but nobody at home had asked to see it. His mom and dad had never once asked how it was played. All they ever said was that it was "going to rot your brain and wreck your eyes."

The old man and the boy stood there for a good three minutes. They were great actors. Both of them. The eighty-three-year-old feigning prolonged interest in Zelda, a dimly animated character on a screen half the size of his palm, and the thirteen-year-old, using his deep radio-announcer voice, pretending this was purely a man-to-man scientific explanation of high-tech wizardry.

"That's sure something," said his grandpa with approval. "Did you know your shirt collar's crooked?"

He folded down the collar, patted the boy's back, and said, "That's a real nice shirt you have there."

The boy paused, looked at this man seventy years his senior, a man two generations and a lifestyle removed, and said, "Did you know flannel is in? Your shirt's pretty cool, too."

OF GERSHWIN AND PICKLES

A quart of kosher dill, Polish dill, and bread and butter pickles have adorned my kitchen countertop for more than a month now. I don't leave them out hoping friends and guests will mistakenly believe I am a talented home canner (however, if they made such an erroneous assumption, I'd probably take my sweet time correcting it). They sit as a reminder that some people still take pride in their work.

The gifted home canner is a thirty-six-year-old construction worker. He is also my brother, a big fella whose knuckles and knees are calloused from crawling on floors laying tile to blueprint specifications. He often stays a little late to fix other people's haphazard work and bring a job up to his standards. When work is over, he, his wife, and two boys drive out to a stretch of meadow where they hope to build a house one day. Until the house becomes a financial reality, they putter around the land, tending a huge garden, often toting home several five-gallon buckets of cucumbers at a time.

He hauls cucumbers into the kitchen, where each one is uniformly sliced and meticulously aligned in a jar like the Royal Palace Guards standing at attention. The Polish dill are garnished with a splash of red pimento and the bread and butter nestle among mustard seeds and onion slices, all of equal length.

These pickles are a work of art with state fair potential. But that's not why he does it. The pickles are not about winning blue ribbons. They're about the joy of working with one's hands and the satisfaction of accomplishment.

It's funny how a job well done can ignite in others a desire to try something new—or simply try harder. Inspiration often comes in unexpected forms from unexpected places. Sometimes it's in the beauty of simplicity, the way morning sun rays set frosted leaves to sparkling, the way a fly ball drops perfectly into an outstretched glove, or the way a primary student forms a perfect lowercase letter *b*.

Sometimes inspiration is more complex; it's the challenge of tackling the truly knotty and unraveling it one thread at a time. I caught a glimpse of that type of inspiration talking to a pianist who was preparing for a Gershwin concert.

She was concerned about the interpretation of the second movement of one of Gershwin's "Three Preludes." "There's always been some question as to how fast the second movement should be played. There's a great opportunity for *rubato*, but how much do you take?" she asked.

Good question. And an even better question: What is *rubato*? It sounded like one of those brightly colored wine cooler drinks, but I knew better.

She continued, "Gershwin played rapidly and without a lot of pedaling on his more popular music, so you don't want to use a lot of pedal. You want to keep it crystal clear so it doesn't sound like a ballad or a concerto. When he wrote his more romantic pieces and some heavy-duty pieces, like "Concerto in F" and probably "Rhapsody in Blue," those you approach more as a concert pianist. But I think you have to have more of a ragtime mentality when you play the other."

It was wonderful to listen to someone discussing technicalities that I didn't know a whit about. It was inspiring to listen to an artist consumed by her craft, determined to understand every single detail and to reach as close to perfection as possible.

Pickles and Gershwin are odd bedfellows, but together they deliver a deadly blow to the ugly notion that all Americans are lazy—that we have all become a people content with producing second-rate goods and slipshod materials.

The truth is, a lot of people still take pride in their work. For many, excellence will always be the goal. I know it's true. I've eaten the pickles and listened to the Gershwin that prove it.

EDISON, EINSTEIN, AND TWITS

English is my first language. Naturally, I assumed English would be my children's first language, too. But something's wrong. They don't seem to understand a word I say.

I say, "Hurry, I smell smoke," and they walk at the speed of a garden slug with mono. I say, "Hush, you're pushing Grandma into the stroke range," and thirty seconds later one of them screams, "ATTACK," as he lunges from a closet with a bow and arrow. I say, "Wear something nice today," and find them pawing through a box of old clothes destined for the rag bag.

They march to their own beat—I think it's rap. They refuse to fit into my preconceived molds and do not share my reverence for organization, cleanliness, and efficiency.

They hoard biologically degradable things under their beds and find nothing disgusting about big wads of dried toothpaste clinging to the bathroom sink. And this is what I'm supposed to mold into responsible, intelligent adults?

I'm a desperate woman in need of encouragement.

I found it in an unlikely spot—a compilation of biographies. My kids think we're learning about famous people and their deeds. What we're really learning is that mothers who nurtured grubbed-out, eccentric, waltzing-on-a-moonbeam kind of children without crushing their spirits, have actually been able to remember their phone numbers after only three shock treatments. Consider the following:

He may have won international prizes for his work in physics, but as a kid there was no way Albert Einstein would ever be voted "best dressed." He rarely wore socks and thought personal grooming was a waste of time. He was into big hair long before the patents were issued on mousse and blow dryers.

If you want contrary, peek into the childhood of the painter Georgia O'Keeffe. When her sisters wore their hair up, she insisted on wearing hers down. When they wore their hair down, she wore hers up. She was a "detail queen" who could swear to the color and pattern of someone's dress she saw when she was less than two years old.

What about the small boy who would languish in the yard for hours staring at blades of grass only inches from his face? His distraught mother thought his eyesight was poor and took him to the doctor. His eyes were great. Ernst Haas gained worldwide fame for his photographs—many of them beautifully composed close-ups of nature.

Thomas Alva Edison's mother stewed and fretted when her twelve-year-old son asked permission to earn extra money by selling concessions on a train to Detroit. She finally consented, only to find the boy couldn't hold on to a dime. He blew every cent he earned on his boyhood hobby—chemistry.

As a child, author Louisa May Alcott loved to pull the biggest books off the shelves in her father's study and build houses and bridges. Once she built a tower around her baby sister, Lizzie, and ran off to play outdoors. Eventually the family found Lizzie asleep in her cellblock of books.

Tired of hounding your eight-year-old about the dirt caked under his nails? That's how old George Washington

186

Carver was when he'd sneak out to his little plot of soil at 4 A.M. to begin "experimenting." Carver became an agricultural chemist who invented three hundred products using chemicals from the peanut.

Teddy Roosevelt's mother was a patient woman. She tolerated the seal's skull and other "finds" Teddy brought home. But even she lost her cool when he gave shelter to a family of white mice in her refrigerator.

As a blooming musician in his late teens, Duke Ellington's parents more than once requested he play "Just Outside the Door" when he'd break out in syncopated melodies they thought unbecoming to middle-class blacks.

And take Mark Twain—please—even for an afternoon. It would have given his mother a well-deserved break. She said, "He was more of a trial than all of the other children put together."

I appreciate the varied contributions these talented people have made to our world—the electric lightbulb, chunky peanut butter, and watercolors of oriental poppies. But today, I salute these great Americans for being twits as kids. It gives me hope.

HOME ALONE

There's a world of difference between quiet and empty. Quiet is the blissful sound of children taking afternoon naps—it's an audible, treasured peace. Empty is the thumping of a solitary heartbeat and the echo of one lone voice in a house.

For the first time in eleven years, our house feels empty. Our "baby" has entered first grade. All three kids are gone all day now, until 2:42 P.M. to be precise. It's just me. Home alone.

I'm no longer the mother of a kindergarten student, preschool kid, or toddler. Cookie Monster and Mr. Rogers won't be stopping by on PBS. It's past time to take the safety plugs out of the electrical outlets and bid farewell to preschool carpools. There'll be no slathering shaving cream on the kitchen counter to create wild and wonderful art before 9 A.M. Raffi needn't serenade me anymore while I'm doing errands. But I can't give up the lullaby tape:

> *I like your eyes;*
> *I like your nose;*
> *I like your mouth,*
> *Your ears, your hands, your toes.*
> *I like your face*
> *It's really you;*
> *There's no one else exactly like you.*

It seems like only yesterday that melody was playing during middle-of-the-night feedings. I can still smell the sweet scent of their newborn skin and see the variation of color in each baby's eyes. Time stands still for mommas with babes in their arms.

Then you blink twice, and your little people have mastered rolling over and sitting up. They've kicked off their booties and slid into laceless high-tops overnight. The cute little T-shirts branded "I love Mom" have vanished—replaced by tank tops with a cocky, lime-green stegosaurus riding on a surfboard and brandishing an electric guitar. Before you can say "immunization records," they've swapped their training pants for Batman and Barbie lunch boxes and headed off to school.

BRR-UM! they're gone. Just like the big yellow school bus in the Little Golden Book *Cars and Trucks*, they disappear with a roar. I thought this day would never come.

For more than a decade, the boundaries of my life have largely been this house and a three-mile radius that includes the grocery store, the pediatrician, and the preschool. We've had fun days of playing, silliness, exploring, and wonderment. We've also had days where the fur flew as we've fought like tomcats staking out territory. There have been days I wondered about the freedoms that were outside my front door. And at times, I yearned for the door to open— just a crack.

The first breeze seemed to dry the spit-up trailing down my shoulder and soothe the frustrations of communicating with preverbal creatures. Gradually, the door opened farther with each milestone the children passed: eating table food, potty training, making their own beds, riding their bikes without training wheels.

Suddenly, the door was ajar far enough they could all shove past me to catch the school bus. Mysteriously, the long list of very important and urgent grown-up projects I was panting to get at seems insignificant, if not downright dull.

Maybe it's because I'm savoring the smaller freedoms first. If I want to eat M&Ms and rattle the bag, I can. If I want to grocery shop without someone running the cart over the back of my heels, I can. If I want to leisurely stroll through the crystal department of a department store, I can.

But if I want to snatch those kids back to recapture a few more days of finger painting and building forts with the dining room chairs, I can't. They're past all that now. The door's swung open wide to another season of life.

And if I've said it once, I've said it a million times, "Will someone please shut the door!" It feels a tad chilly in this empty house.

THE BLUEBIRD OF FREEDOM

In every home lies forbidden fruit. In my childhood home, it was a bluebird candy dish perched on the coffee table in the living room. The blue bowl was seven inches in diameter. On top of its lid was a hand-blown bird tilted in descent position. He had a round head, plump, oval body, and a dramatic tail that swooped six inches into the air.

The bluebird was more than a candy dish. It was my mother's small reminder that in this house, children did not rule the roost. It was a symbol of resistance to the often overbearing theme of motherhood. That theme, of course, being Surrender.

From the time babies begin bulging in the womb, women quickly learn motherhood is about surrendering. Initially, you surrender your body: the abdominal muscles first, followed by the breasts upon baby's arrival.

Uninterrupted nights of sleep are surrendered to a schedule that drags you from bed every two to three hours. When baby becomes mobile, even your bathroom routine is intruded upon. Soon, cookies, salad croutons, and bottles of soda are no longer exclusive property. Your purse becomes a community utility bag for diaper rash cream, Bert and Ernie finger puppets, and Cheerios.

Then comes a fork in the road where mothers must choose. Some select the path of least resistance, surrendering all to the children: stereo knobs, sofa cushions, even dress shoes. Other mothers grasp at something tangible and boldly declare, "This is mine. You can't have it. It's off limits to sticky fingers. It will never be buried in the sandbox or lugged to show-and-tell as long as I can breathe!"

The bluebird candy dish was our mother's artifact of choice. My brother and I knew that if we chipped, winged, or otherwise maimed that hunk of blue glass, there would be a mortal price to pay. We planned our lives accordingly. When chasing around the coffee table and swinging at one another in the living room, we were careful to aim a quarter inch above the bird's tail. Naturally, the unspoken question was whose name would be engraved on our mother's heart as the child who shattered her symbol of authority.

There was a close call in 1983 (details are fuzzy, I was living in Oregon) in which my brother allegedly was tidying up the house after a small social gathering he had hosted while my parents were out of town. In my brother's haste, the bird was toppled from its nest, fracturing the tail. Since it happened in the midst of such a noble gesture as dusting—and the bird was repairable—my mother remained mum.

My brother eventually left home as well (not over the bird; he met a nice girl). We both married, had children, returned home for holidays, and rarely chased one another around the coffee table. Instead, our children chased one another around the coffee table. Ever alert, Grandma frequently declared her love for the bluebird to all five grandchildren and recounted its 1983 near-death experience.

I always believed it would be one of my brother's boys who would bear the legacy of destroying the bluebird. After all, the curious tykes disassemble everything within reach and constantly mess with tools. They've had motive and opportunity—they live in the same city as Grandma, not five hundred miles away like my children. Furthermore, my brother's youngest has a prior record. He'd once hurled Grandma's crystal coasters across the living room like Frisbees.

Alas, the winds of change blew and Grandma redecorated the living room. With a twinge of glee we watched the bluebird relocate to a back bedroom.

But a new symbol of power took its place—an exquisite crystal candy dish. This lid featured a sparkling three-inch piece of glass that soared toward the heavens like a church steeple. Grandma, in predictable fashion, declared her love for the new candy dish, her hope that it would live a long life and basked in its beauty.

The long awaited disaster struck Saturday. Someone was fiddling with a stuck lock on the patio door. Abruptly turning to reach for a tool near the coffee table, the dish was smashed to smithereens. It was more than the death of a candy dish. It was the end of an icon that sat as a tribute to the fact that children do not rule all households. It was a symbol of personhood beyond motherhood.

Oddly enough, it wasn't my brother, nor myself, nor our children, who were responsible for the ultimate deed of destruction.

Tough break, Dad.

Epilogue

My better half and I recently came home, after a Saturday night out, to a frightening scenario. We walked into a clean and tidy kitchen. Our hearts racing, we immediately called out to the kids. One by one, they calmly answered from their quiet bedrooms.

Before I had kids, I would not have questioned the legitimacy of a scene like that. Before I was a mother, I would have thought such a scenario entirely plausible and reasonable. I was naive enough to believe three kids might actually spend a Saturday night in their bedrooms organizing their underwear drawers, reviewing notes for history class, or reading the label on a shampoo bottle.

But now, after earning my stripes as the mother of three and having seventeen years of on-the-job training under my belt, I know better. I know when you come home to a clean kitchen and a quiet house with three adolescents, something is afoul.

"What do you think is wrong?" I asked, clutching at my husband's arm.

"Hopefully, nothing big," he said. "Don't panic. There's no need to go off the deep end."

"What do you mean, don't panic?" I hissed. "Look around. The refrigerator door is shut. There isn't a bloated corn dog or sign of nachos in the microwave. There's not a dirty dish in sight."

As a matter of fact, the kitchen was spotless. I was beginning to hyperventilate.

"I see what you mean," he said, a look of concern now spreading over his face as well.

"Listen," I said, "do you hear it?"

"Your rapid, shallow breathing?" he asked.

"No. Do you hear *it*?"

"What?" he said.

"Nothing. No television, no radio, no stereo. This is really scaring me," I said.

"Yeah, and no one is hanging on the phone either," he said, breaking into a cold sweat himself.

We rounded the corner to the family room and I immediately patted the back of the television set. Stone cold. What's more, the remote was laying neatly on top of the VCR. Something was wrong, really wrong.

"Look! Over there!" my husband cried, pointing to two eighteen-inch black heel marks on the hardwood floor.

"Yes!" I said feeling a surge of hope and optimism. "And the cushions on the sofa are all askew."

"Yes!" he said, smiling broadly. "And look at that, pop cans by the fireplace mantle and an empty bag of Jolly Ranchers in the seat of the overstuffed chair. The coffee table is shoved up against the bookshelves, the lampshade is crooked, and shoes and socks are all over the floor."

"What a relief," I sighed.

"I told you not to panic," he said. "Everything's fine. Obviously, they've been chasing each other through the house like maniacs and wrestling in the living room. They must have heard the garage door go up and scattered. Feel better now?" my husband asked.

"Much," I said with a smile, "much."

ACKNOWLEDGMENTS

Many of the ideas in this book germinated years ago as my own mom and dad modeled the commitment, sacrifice, and sense of humor it takes to build a family. I am grateful to my parents, Ken and Virginia Borgman, along with my in-laws, Herbert and the late Oma Nye, for their love and support as well as being the best public relations team this side of the Atlantic. They have routinely thrust photocopies of my newspaper column into the hands of virtual strangers throughout the Midwest.

Among the friends and colleagues I owe a debt of thanks to are: Frank Caperton and Ted Daniels at *The Indianapolis Star,* for giving my column a home; my editor Ruth Holladay, who has been a steady source of encouragement; Mike Duggan at the Knight Ridder Tribune News Service for giving my newspaper column an opportunity for national distribution; Diana Larson and Ruth Ann Gantz for being reliable sounding boards; and my many friends at Zionsville Fellowship for the spirited and lively exchange of ideas.

I also wish to thank Mary Tahan of Clausen, Mays and Tahan Literary Agency for believing this book was possible, and Mitchell Ivers of Pocket Books for realizing that Mary was absolutely right.

Finally, I am profoundly grateful to my husband, Charlie Nye, for being my front-line editor and for having the courage to tell me what does and doesn't work. We are still married.

ABOUT THE AUTHOR

LORI BORGMAN's humor column on parenting and family life is nationally distributed by Knight Ridder Tribune News Service. She has worked as a photojournalist and a news editor. Her credentials include bags under her eyes and the ability to whip up dinner for five with just a pound of pasta, a half-stick of butter, and a box of broccoli with a nasty case of freezer burn. She lives with her husband and children in Indianapolis, Indiana.